MURDER & CRIME

WHITECHAPEL & DISTRICT

THE ILLUSTRATED POLICE NEWS

LAW COURTS,
AND WEEKLY RECORD
ESTABLISHED 1864

No. 1816. [REGISTERED FOR CIRCULATION IN THE UNITED KINGDOM AND ABROAD.] SATURDAY, DEC. 3, 1898. Price One Pe

ANOTHER WHITECHAPEL HORROR NEAR THE
SCENE OF A "RIPPER" CRIME

MURDER & CRIME

WHITECHAPEL & DISTRICT

M.W. OLDRIDGE

The
History
Press

This book is dedicated to Mum, Dad, Emma, Philip, David, and Lucas

Frontispiece: Illustrated Police News, 8 December 1898, courtesy of Robert Clack.

First published 2011

The History Press
The Mill, Brimscombe Port
Stroud, Gloucestershire, GL5 2QG
www.thehistorypress.co.uk

British Library Cataloguing in Publication Data.
A catalogue record for this book is available from the British Library.

ISBN 978 0 7524 5549 5

Typesetting and origination by The History Press
Manufacturing managed by Jellyfish Print Solutions Ltd.
Printed in India

CONTENTS

INTRODUCTION

Whitechapel and Spitalfields have not yet shed their reputation as the gloomy headquarters of Victorian crime – and they probably never will. Jack the Ripper, from beyond his (I suppose) uncelebrated grave, sees to that, although the nature of his crimes marks him out as uncharacteristic, rather than typical, of nineteenth-century transgression. He is a little cottage industry of his own, and, for the clutches of folk who visit the area after dark, touring in his invisible footsteps, a commodity to be traded nightly in the streets of the East End. The deal, to be specific, involves the telling of the guide's ghastly story of ghostly, gas-lamp-lit times on the one hand, and the safe return of the audience to their tube station, for example, at the end of the tour on the other. Jack the Ripper is a gruesome universe one visits; but obviously one never stays there.

To many late Victorian and Edwardian Londoners, Whitechapel and Spitalfields were equally obscure places, as foreign as if they were overseas. The boundaries of the City of London, the Empire's affluent seat of commercial interests, were made of glass, and the ruling classes were loath to make the journey to the other side. In the early 1900s, the American writer Jack London confounded the staff of the Cheapside branch of Thomas Cook's travel agency. He wished to see the East End – a matter of minutes' walk away – but discovered that his advisers were better equipped to send him to 'Darkest Africa or Innermost Thibet'. They considered his wish to sojourn in London's most dangerous, dismal, depraved and destitute manors 'unusual', even 'unprecedented'. At worst, they interpreted the plan as a particularly perverse kind of suicide. There was no guarantee, then, that the tourist would return.

Of course, in some ways, the East End was foreign – or, better, the East End was foreign to some extent, and in some parts. It had for many years been peopled, in part, by successive waves of newly-arrived immigrants, and, throughout the period covered by the cases in this book, the dominant non-indigenous community was Ashkenazi Jewish. Chased from Eastern Europe by brutal and intolerant regimes, hundreds of thousands of Jewish refugees filed into Whitechapel and Spitalfields in the late Victorian and Edwardian periods. With

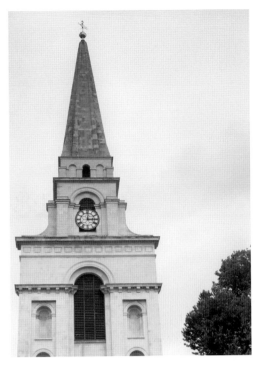

Unmoved above the local destitution: Christ Church, Spitalfields. (Author's collection)

them, they often brought skills and a sense of endeavour; some others brought radical socialism; and some encountered the law, as demonstrated by some of the stories contained herein. Alongside the Jewish communities, an amalgam of the destitute from all over the United Kingdom and Ireland was formed as the nation's poorest people gravitated inexorably to East London. This section of the population, too, kept the police busy, as their desperation pushed them into conflict with statute. Along the main roads, it was true, some artisans and merchants maintained a comparatively salubrious existence, but even these groups were not immune to lapses into crime, as the first case in this book illustrates.

Beyond those covered here, there are other crimes for which Whitechapel and Spitalfields are renowned. Occurring to the south of the district, the Ratcliff Highway murders of 1811 once gripped the nation; to the east, a century later, so did the Sidney Street Siege, and I touch on this case only in passing. More recently, the Krays painted themselves indelibly and rather redly into the area's criminal landscape – the murder of George Cornell took place in the Blind Beggar in 1966, and the twins' dubious influence on the East End was once commemorated cheerfully in the games room of that establishment. Then, under new management, a post-millennial shame seemed to kick in, and the memorabilia vanished from around the pool table; now, their portrait has been restored to the pub's promotional material. Things change. The interested reader can find more details about all of these crimes in many other books.

This is a version of Jack London's journey in miniature; an excursion to the dark heart of the Victorian and Edwardian no-place located on the edge of riches. It is possible only because of the much-appreciated support, assistance, and guidance of the following people: John Bennett, Rob Clack, Nick Connell, Paul Daniel, Stewart Evans, Liza Hopkinson, Cate Ludlow, Matilda Richards, Neil R. Storey, and R.L. Wright.

M.W. Oldridge, 2011

One

1874

The limelight washes over the immense frame of the Tichborne Claimant. From the stage, he gazes out into the darkness of the Pavilion Theatre, Whitechapel. He scrutinises any face he picks out in the gloom. Here, he sees conviction; here, faith; there, and there, and there, incredulity. He reassures himself with the thought of the profits of the performance, by the terms of his agreement uncoupled to the confidence of the crowd. Another wave for the blackness before him. Another smile forced across the famous jowls.

The Tichborne Claimant – a great hulk of a man, once known in Australia as Thomas Castro, and before that, apparently, as Wapping butcher Arthur Orton – purports to be the lost son of a rich dowager. He parodies the physical features of the missing man, the wiry, frail Roger Tichborne. He is unblessed by Roger's lackadaisical erudition; cannot recall any detail of his schooldays at Stoneyhurst, remembering only Winchester; tells tales of rank-and-file petty heroism, though Roger was a commissioned officer. He does not square with the facts. But his romantic narrative has attracted England's ready devotion, and some have even pinned their colours to the mast. For them, the Claimant is Roger Tichborne, returned from his watery grave, shipwrecked off the coast of South America. Some – here, and here; another podgy salute sent into the Pavilion's shadows – some take this view. And one of the most devout adherents to this unlikely position is the old dowager herself.

But the law has already begun to gain on the Claimant, and now he tours the theatres, bringing out supporters and nay-sayers alike in an attempt to fund his defence against a forgery charge. Perspiration drips from his anxious face after another draining public rehearsal of his dubious credentials. Still he fixes his gaze on the crowd in the Pavilion. Above him, the drop curtain unexpectedly falls, weighted at the bottom, threatening to end the drama in a surreal, ugly moment of carelessness from the wings. It will shatter his skull – he is directly beneath it – and the main attraction does not notice its rapid descent.

Then, from the crowd, a bearded figure springs forward, moderately tall, broad-shouldered, powerful enough, and the Claimant is bundled out of the way of the plummeting curtain. It misses him, misses his rescuer, and after a moment's pause, the Claimant bulges through

The exterior of the Royal Pavilion Theatre, as Wainwright would have remembered it from his childhood. (*The Illustrated London News*, 23 February 1856)

the curtain and stands centre-front to receive the cheers of the masses; unhurt, alive, and hand in hand with sharp-eyed Mr Henry Wainwright.

★

Wainwright himself had generated a little local profile through the years. He had lived in the East End all his life, initially on the Whitechapel Road, the eldest son of Henry William Wainwright and his wife Elizabeth. Henry *père* made his way as a brushmaker, by 1851 employing thirty men in his factory at 84 Whitechapel Road, adjacent to the Pavilion Theatre. Henry *fils* rapidly outshone him, inheriting the trade and, by the early 1870s, more than trebling the workforce. With his wife and young family, he decamped east to luxurious Tredegar Square in Bow, a measure of the man's prosperity and respectability. He cut a prepossessing figure in society: in the flush of his thirties, fourteen – perhaps fifteen – stones in weight, his countenance adorned with a copious beard, jovial and gregarious by nature, he was, in sum, mesmeric to women. The classic portrait of Wainwright emphasises his wavy hair and his mouth, puckered into a serious aspect, which I cheerfully follow countless previous writers on the man in describing as 'sensual'.

Wainwright likewise acquired all the social contacts suitable to a man of his position and class. He patronised the local churches, threw himself energetically into charitable works and aligned himself with the policies of the Conservative Party. He exhibited a fascination for the thespian *demi-monde* of the Pavilion, and would invite actresses to supper, forcing them to sit through his wooden-ish post-prandial rendition of Thomas Hood's true-crime poem *The Dream of Eugene Aram*. Later, out of sight of his wife, he would seduce them, too, sparing no expense in his pursuit of the ephemeral female stars of Whitechapel's stage. This was the moral flaw behind the principled exterior, but Wainwright's reputation consistently resisted any attempts to sink it, and, as the 1860s became the 1870s, he hunted opportunities for pleasure – social, sexual and otherwise salacious – with increasingly cynical zeal.

The queue for the London Pavilion at the turn of the century.

A trip to the Broxbourne Gardens, then a renowned place of resort for the city-weary East Londoner, appears to have been the catalyst of Wainwright's demise. In 1871, he encountered there one Harriet Louisa Lane, a striking nineteen-year-old (or thereabouts), the youngest of nine daughters born to an aspiring engineer who had abandoned life in Weymouth in favour of the gas facilities of north Middlesex. Harriet herself emerged from this middlingly-respectable background with limited ambitions, a little skill in millinery and small, delicate hands, with fingers in neat proportion. She also had a decayed tooth which was visible when she laughed or smiled, and a scar on her right leg caused by a childhood burn. Whether or not she scintillated in Broxbourne is hard to know, but Wainwright, seeing her, was apparently smitten. By the July of that year, he was referring to her in a letter as 'Darling creature', and, before the end of the year, 'My little Beauty'. The conventional nature of these lovestruck exchanges was only marred by Wainwright's insistence on the adoption of pseudonyms: hers, Miss L. Varco; his, George Williams, later George Varco. He demanded that the foundation of respectability upon which his public persona was built should remain untouched by this new romantic venture.

Still, matters advanced. A European tour (perhaps enforced by his business interests, and perhaps not) whirled Wainwright out of Harriet's life, whirling him back in some months later with fresh declarations of affection, and a new *nom de guerre*. He was now Mr Percy King, with all its ostentatious and even ribald undertones, and she Mrs King. The fictitious union was announced in the press, through a paid advertisement submitted, it is said, in a female hand. It may be that, with her twentieth birthday approaching, a more confident and mature Harriet had decided to steer the sightless ship herself. Percy – formerly Varco and Williams, and properly Henry Wainwright – went along with the conceit. He installed her in rooms in St Peter's Street, Mile End, a brisk walk from his business in one direction, and from the residence of his neglected wife and family in the other. In August 1872, Beatrice Wainwright King, Harriet's first child, was born.

Wainwright divided himself between his interests and his commitments with indifferent success. It did not take long for Harriet's landladies to notice that their tenant's putative husband was scarcely present, and never able to stay the night. Wainwright brushed observations of this sort aside – he was a traveller in business, he said, and was often away from home. But, privately, he seems to have had occasional trouble controlling Harriet: first he moved her to Alfred Place, near the Tottenham Court Road, and then to Cecil Street, off the Strand, and one suspects that, in the background, Harriet's frustrations were beginning to rise. Wainwright cautiously put a degree of distance between his chafing not-wife and the decent public existence to the pretence of which he remained devoted, bringing Harriet back to the East End only when she became pregnant again. Her confinement seems to have acted as a brake on her feelings, and her second daughter was born at St Peter's Street in December 1873. With so much to distract him, however, Wainwright's legitimate business began to sour, and money became scarcer.

Another matter which competed for Wainwright's attention was his resurrected relationship with his younger brother, Thomas. A different physical specimen, slighter, and sporting a wispy moustache, Thomas had, by his own admission, fallen out of favour with his family, until 'one Saturday in March 1874' – in fact, the day of the Boat Race, won by Cambridge by three-and-a-half lengths – when he encountered Henry in Fenchurch Street. They drank, Thomas revealed that he had found a position working for Mr Arkell of

The inherent vulgarity of the Tichborne Claimant was hardly concealed by his shammed nobility.

Lady Tichborne, self-deluded, devoted to her unlikely fantasy.

291 Oxford Street, an ironmonger and cutler, and they parted on good terms. A few weeks passed, and then Henry began to appear at Thomas's workplace, inveigling Thomas into apparently harmless complicity in several of his more trivial financial arrangements – bills to be defrayed, and that sort of thing. He would arrive, Thomas said, at dinner time, and 'on three occasions he brought Alice Day with him'.

Alice was the heiress apparent to Harriet's unenviable position. She was a ballet dancer orbiting the airless community of the Pavilion, and though she was adamant that 'there was never the slightest impropriety' between them, it seems likely that she and Wainwright had tumbled into casual sexual acquaintance long since. In May 1874, Harriet, full of complaints, again was moved by Wainwright into lodgings at 3 Sidney Square, to be overseen by Jemima Foster, the landlady, while Wainwright himself visited less and less. She was being marginalised, and the looming figure of Alice Day, poised to fill a vacuum which Wainwright's selfish nature abhorred, did not escape her notice.

And so things became still more hectic, and the pressure on Wainwright increased. Harriet's dissatisfaction grew louder, and his creditors' patience wore thinner. The high-premium expectations of life at Tredegar Square had begun to bite, and Wainwright later moved his family from Bow to Chingford – they were reported to be living there 'in a very humble way'. But, as early as September 1874, and to Wainwright's manifest alarm, the fractures in the social facade had become unavoidably apparent. Something happened to tip Harriet over the edge, and, one evening, her friend and the sometime nanny to her children, Ellen Wilmore, found her outside her Sidney Square lodgings, 'intoxicated and excited'. Ellen brought Harriet in, sat with her and calmed her; but the next day Jemima Foster told Harriet that she had to go, and offered her only a couple of days' grace on account of Harriet's obvious lack of funds. Ellen helped Harriet to pack her scant belongings into boxes, and, on Friday 11 September 1874, at four o'clock in the afternoon, Harriet Lane stepped into the East End's autumn air.

★

Wainwright's rapidly folding empire still, at this time, took in two premises, both on the Whitechapel Road: number 84, previously mentioned, and, almost directly opposite it, number 215. The latter was a narrow, deep affair, extending a hundred yards back, and with an off-street entrance via nearby Vine Court. His name, worth less than ever, was emblazoned over the front. That summer, Harriet had made an awkward habit of confronting him there while he affected nonchalance, divorcing himself emotionally from a sham marriage to a girl whom he had begun to realise was hardly the pushover he had hoped she would be. Now, homeless and forced to desperate means, she went there again, no doubt expecting to be able to demand that her husband throw more money at her. Since he had become a failure in business, the last thing left for Wainwright to purchase was Harriet's silence.

Unfortunately, Mrs Foster's kindness to Harriet – two days' notice on the tenancy – had had the effect of concentrating Wainwright's distracted mind. On 10 September, the day before his *inamorata* was to take leave of her rooms, he had ordered half a hundredweight of chloride of lime to be delivered to him; elsewhere, he kept a revolver which he had tried unsuccessfully

Edward Frieake. (Courtesy of R.L. Wright)

to pawn in June, and a rope. When Harriet arrived at his shop, all fire and fury, he shot her through the head, cut her throat for good measure, and dragged her with the rope into a rudimentary grave he had prepared at the back of the premises. Upon her body he heaped the chloride of lime, expecting it to dissolve the remains; and he closed the grave; and there things rested, the instant explosion of noise of the gunshot giving way to the very silence for which Wainwright had long prayed, but which, penny for penny, he could no longer afford.

The critical mass of Wainwright's economic collapse resisted even the elimination of Harriet, however. It was too late to prevent his business going up in smoke – literally, since in November 1874, there was a mysterious fire at 84 Whitechapel Road, in which the building, which had been in Wainwright's family for decades, was utterly ruined. Legend had it that thoughtful fire-watchers had bravely rescued Wainwright's ledgers from the flames. These betrayed his parlous financial position, although he might have been happy for them to have burned, and, when he came to apply for the insurance on his wrecked property, the Sun Fire Office withheld the payout. There were the inevitable suspicions of arson, against which Wainwright protested noisily, if not plausibly. He took out an action against the company, and joined the great procession of charlatans – his own hero, the disputed Roger Tichborne, among them – filing slowly through the Victorian courts.

In the absence of the expected insurance windfall, Wainwright scrabbled for funds. Thomas, his prodigal brother, set up an aligned ironmongery business in Borough, the other side of London Bridge, which imploded almost instantly. Queries about the whereabouts of Harriet Lane began to roll in, testing Wainwright's resolve. Ellen Wilmore, who had, months before, watched her, head held high against her predicament, leaving Sidney Square, westbound for the Whitechapel Road, received unlikely assurances that Harriet had taken off for the continent with a man by the unusual name of Edward Frieake. Wilmore had

The site of Wainwright's shop at 215 Whitechapel Road. (Author's collection)

The rear of Wainwright's shop at 215 Whitechapel Road. (Author's collection)

wondered at this – it hardly seemed likely, given Harriet's situation in September 1874 – and, gradually, Frieake himself, an auctioneer working at Aldgate, became aware of the story. He encountered little trouble tracing the rumour to Wainwright. Frieake – his name pronounced in the German fashion, with three syllables – had been acquainted with Wainwright for, he estimated, 'twelve or fourteen years,' and went right away to confront him with the injudicious lie. Wainwright was all wide-eyes and earnest reassurance.

'Oh, Teddy, old man,' said Wainwright. 'It is not you; it is another Teddy Frieake.'

'Well,' objected Frieake, 'it is a very serious imputation to cast upon my character, and should it get to the ears of the lady I am engaged to be married to, it will very likely ruin my happiness.'

Besides this, Frieake had considered the probability of there being, indeed, another version of himself. 'If I had met another Henry Wainwright, and been introduced to him, I should have asked him whether he had any relations in Whitechapel,' he commented, pointing out that, 'mine is not a Brown, Jones, or Robinson name.' This logic seemed impeccable. And yet, curious to tell, there had indeed been a visit to 3 Sidney Square, Harriet's former home, by a man introduced as Mr Frieake, while she was yet living there. Ellen Wilmore had seen this *alter*-Frieake, and so had Jemima Foster. But it was not Edward, whose photograph, taken years before, depicts him in full, proud, bearded manhood. Even Henry Wainwright accepted that the man who had whisked Harriet away, and, by extension, the one who had visited her at Sidney Square, had been 'only a young fellow about twenty-three or twenty-four, with a slight, black moustache'. This was a remarkable physical match for the enigmatic Thomas, and telegrams from the coast which seemed to confirm Wainwright's tale of Harriet's elopement were sent, it was later discovered, by Thomas, via a helpful train guard.

★

Wainwright finally crumbled into official bankruptcy in June 1875, and found work at Edward Martin's corn chandlery in New Road. Although he was appointed manager of one of Martin's three stores, the dissolution of his own business must have rankled with him. Later, it was possible for a newspaper to write that Wainwright 'was held to be a most respectable man' in Whitechapel, with the emphasis distinctly on the 'was'. This was a fall from grace of an inescapably public variety.

Worse would follow, however, if 215 Whitechapel Road was given up for mortgage against Wainwright's debts. Although he no longer traded from the premises, he had kept a key. A solicitor named Samuel Behrend — to whom Wainwright owed money — had claimed the lease after the bankruptcy of the former owner, and had installed temporary tenants through the summer months. Wainwright called cheerily (although perhaps a little too often) in order to collect his mail. The tenants suspected nothing; word had it that a dog which had made itself an *habitué* of the second entrance to the warehouse, in Vine Court, had mysteriously disappeared. Against all of this, the smell which permeated the so-called paint shop — the room at the back of the premises where the floor was boarded with wood, rather than laid with flagstones — was becoming intolerable. When it was noticed by customers and visitors, Wainwright would attribute the stench to heaps of rubbish and rotting cabbages; but privately, he wondered that half a hundredweight of chloride of lime seemed not to have eradicated the body of Harriet Lane. If it had, he reasoned, her nauseating scent would not have advertised her whereabouts; it was only good fortune which had prevented any of the summer's occupants from ripping up the floorboards to isolate the cause of the pollution. When Behrend advertised the empty property for sale at the start of September 1875, his last short-term tenants having moved away, Wainwright knew that his opportunities to access the property were finite and, almost a year on from her interment, he now planned to remove Harriet from her makeshift tomb.

This was a predictably grisly affair. Wainwright bought some American oilcloth, a chopper and a shovel, entered the temporarily-empty building some time after hours

Wainwright's hammer and cleaver, the tools of his grisly surgery.

on Friday 10 September 1875, dug up the remains of Harriet Lane, and disarticulated her, packing her separated sections (of which there were apparently ten) into two parcels wrapped in the oilcloth. Having mistaken chloride of lime, a partial preservative of the human frame, for quicklime (which consumes it), Wainwright discovered Harriet in a state of disarmingly good repair. Far from disappearing, she had merely degraded rather slowly. Wainwright toiled, thwacking the chopper down through the corpse, scoring his desperation into the flagstones nearer the front of the shop – he had dragged the exhumed body there in order to obtain suitable resistance against his urgent blows. The floorboards over Harriet's former resting place he attempted to replace; the bloodstains on the marked stones he covered with ashes. The cloth packages, which now emitted an awful smell, he covered, for the time being, with a veil of straw. Harriet was ready for shipment.

There now followed perhaps the greatest pursuit scene in Victorian criminal history. Wainwright went, on the afternoon of Saturday 11 September, to Alfred Stokes, a twenty-five-year-old casualty of Wainwright's own commercial failure, who had also found work at Martin's on New Road.

'Will you carry a parcel for me, Stokes?' asked Wainwright.

'Yes, sir, with the greatest of pleasure,' replied the deferential Stokes, and, put shortly, Wainwright and Stokes repaired to 215 Whitechapel Road, got into the premises through the Vine Court entrance, collected the parcels (Wainwright taking the lighter of the two), exited again through Vine Court to the Whitechapel Road, and struggled up towards St Mary's Church, where Stokes put his parcel down, complaining that it was too heavy for him, and stank in a most alarming way. Wainwright told Stokes to mind the cargo while he went to fetch a cab from the rank a little way off in Whitechapel High Street. Shifting Harriet would require horse-driven transport.

In Wainwright's absence, Stokes's healthy curiosity got the better of him. It had all been rather strange so far – Wainwright had been ultra-cautious about moving the parcels out of Vine Court while nobody was watching – and the smell which was emanating from the packages Stokes could only describe as 'frightful'. He opened one of the parcels and saw a hand, and a wrist, and then only space where the arm ought to have been. Speaking metaphorically and in retrospect, Stokes described his hair standing on end with such sudden force that his hat was dislodged; in practice, however, he simply closed the package, swallowed his adrenaline, and adopted an attitude of simple dispassion in time for Wainwright's return. Wainwright had found a cab, and together he and Stokes loaded Harriet into the compartment, where Wainwright took a seat next to her and directed the driver to turn through Church Lane into the Commercial Road. He looked down at Stokes and promised to see him back in Whitechapel at seven o'clock that evening. 'All right, sir,' said Stokes, betraying nothing.

The cab pulled away, and Stokes stalked it to the junction of Greenfield Street. Here it stopped, and Wainwright alighted to help Alice Day, the ballet dancer then much in his affections, into the compartment; she would take a drive with him, she said, so long as she was back by a quarter past six. By now, Wainwright was puffing on a great cigar in an attempt to disguise the smell of the awful packages. He gave Day a newspaper to read, and asked her not to interrupt him while he was thinking; he ordered the cab driver to make haste for London Bridge and the Borough. All the while, Stokes hid in a nearby doorway.

An open-air service in Yiddish at St Mary's, Whitechapel, where Stokes rested with his awful parcel.

Above: Thomas Wainwright's business was here, at what was then the 'Hen and Chickens': the low, white building in the centre of the photograph. (Author's collection)

Right: The basement of the former Hen and Chickens. (Author's collection)

The cab turned, and gained speed. Along the Commercial Road, through Whitechapel High Street and Aldgate, Stokes, on foot, bravely kept his pace with the horse-powered flight of Henry Wainwright. At the junction of Leadenhall Street, he breathlessly urged two policemen to stop the cab. 'Man, you must be mad,' they laughed, and Stokes had no option but to continue his headlong dash alone. Fenchurch Street, London Bridge, Borough High Street — still the horse kept up, and still Stokes trailed it. And then it halted, thirty or forty yards from the seat of Thomas Wainwright's short-lived ironmongery enterprise of the previous year, which had been briefly situated in a deep-cellared building then known as the Hen and Chickens.

Wainwright got out of the cab, lifted out one of the parcels, and approached the Hen and Chickens. Setting his sections of Harriet down, he took from his pocket the key to the padlock which secured the door, and pushed it open. He took in the first parcel, left it at the top of the stairs leading to the basement, and returned for the second one.

But Stokes had received a better reception from the police in the Borough than he had from those at Leadenhall Street. He told his unlikely story in highlighted form to PC Henry Turner, who was on duty at the corner of St Thomas' Street, and Turner, to his credit, decided that the unusual allegations were worth looking into. He approached the Hen and Chickens, was joined by another policeman named Arthur Cox, and after a couple of fruitless attempts on Wainwright's part to bribe these defenders of the peace — offering them extravagant sums of money, the likes of which he himself had not seen for years — the packages were opened, Harriet spilled out, and Wainwright was arrested. Alice Day, also detained, and palpably miffed by the whole affair, was later released, but not before her unhappy association with her fallen lover had destroyed her own reputation. This, though, was Wainwright's spreading miasma, and it was obvious — to those who would see it — months before the crazed final fling over London Bridge. Alice herself becomes a shadowy figure hereafter, the performer paying for her sins in the wages of obscurity.

★

The trial began in November and concluded in December. It pieced Harriet Lane together, working backwards from the jigsaw puzzle she eventually became, through her lonely year in the grave, through her callous murder, and back, living again, into Henry Wainwright's compromised history. His conviction was inevitable, and the death sentence was passed.

Beside Wainwright in the dock stood his brother Thomas. He had been brought into custody in October, when he might have thought that the crucible — its ingredients all arms and legs — had conveniently bubbled down. But his role in the matter provoked the deepest suspicion. He had, it was obvious, played the role of Frieake while Harriet was still alive, though presumably at Henry's behest. Who had sent the Frieake telegrams after her death, and had procured the key to the empty Hen and Chickens, and passed it to Henry, just at the moment when he needed, rather urgently, to move Harriet's remains to other quarters? The jury considered him an accessory after the fact, and he was sentenced to seven years' imprisonment, regaining his freedom in the summer of 1881 after remissions for good behaviour. Devious though his conduct had been even before Harriet's demise, it appeared that Thomas had had nothing to do with the murder itself; his employer, Mr Arkell, had not missed him on the night in question.

This left only Henry, the remainder of whose story was played out in the gloom of Newgate Prison. Under sentence of imminent death, he continued to protest his innocence, sticking with the story of Harriet's elopement with the unfortunate Frieake. Allowed to confront his brother under significant guard, Henry astonished all concerned by affecting psychotic surprise – 'You are not Frieake, then?' – at Thomas's 'real' identity. Thomas saw through the crazy charade, terminating the conversation with a suitably chilling riposte: 'You are the greatest villain unhung!' But Henry's illogical exhortations of innocence, his fouling of the truth, had failed to impress anyone, or at least anyone who mattered, and he would not remain unhung much longer.

On the morning of 21 December 1875, Henry Wainwright was brought up to Newgate's scaffold by his executioner, Marwood. The prisoner dispensed with his last cigar as the procession made its solemn way towards the noose. He glanced round at the clutch of people, all there by invitation only, who had assembled to watch the hanging.

'Come to see a man die, have you, you curs?' he asked them; but no response to this bitter accusation was noted.

Besides, they had.

The execution of Henry Wainwright. (Supplement to the *Illustrated Police News*, 25 December 1875)

Two

1887

Poisoning is a particular form of crime against the person, with its own characteristics, and its own stereotypes. The very mention of poisoning in Victorian England often triggers a whole range of assumptions – they were all at it, perhaps; devious, cunning, deliberate; adulterating with suspicious substances their rococo dishes and their lost, intense tastes, the meal warm against the noisily frigid bone china of the dining room. The poisons themselves, though we never see them now, trip off the tongue: arsenic, antimony, laudanum, strychnine – the cupboards and nooks of the Victorian household were jammed with them. They turned up in facial emollients, in weedkiller, or were put down to eliminate rats; they were medicinal in small doses, and fatal in larger ones. They represented the failure of a relationship, or the attempt to speed the end of a relationship which no longer satisfied the poisoner; they betokened planning, patience, and, where necessary, great floods of crocodile tears.

Looked at another way, poisoning was the inverse of, say, stabbing, or shooting. Guns and knives damaged their victims from the outside in; poison worked from the inside out. Weapons were quick, and could be spontaneous; poison was rarely immediate in its effects, and a poisoning campaign typically required careful preparation. Stabbings and shootings were unfastidious and messy, and, though the effects of poisoning on the alimentary tract could be messy indeed, there were those times of calm between the squalls during which the patient would be lying in bed, weak, perhaps distressed, but essentially clean. Sometimes they would be cared for by a nurse whose job it was to stave off the worst effects of the victim's mysterious and sudden illness with great doses of patent medicines, most of which were of mysterious composition themselves.

At the intersection of these two different means of murder stood the acids. Part poison, part offensive weapon, they could be introduced to the body through the mouth, but the damage they caused was often gruesome and direct, searing swiftly through the tissues of the throat and the stomach. The optimism of, for example, the aspiring arsenic poisoner was unavailable to the acid killer: the former hoped that the medics performing the autopsy upon the deceased would mistake the symptoms of deliberate poisoning for those of any of a range of naturally-occurring gastric complaints; but the latter knew that their choice of weapon would leave its unambiguous mark. When not given orally, acids doubled as agents of outside-in damage – they could be thrown at others – and they had a range of industrial uses, from the legitimate to the illicit. In the East End, where anybody's bedroom could double as the seat of almost any secondary industry, they were widely available for retail, suiting the requirements of the hand-to-mouth manufacturers of the bric-a-brac of daily life. At the other end of the spectrum, they coloured and discoloured the coins of counterfeiters, who skirted the scrutiny of the usual revenue agencies. Implicit in all of this unregulated, behind-closed-doors activity were the terribly straitened circumstances of the majority, teetering too often into desperation. In such situations, the criminal potential of the acids must, sometimes, have been unhappily obvious.

★

At 16 Batty Street, in the late June of 1887, lived Isaac Angel and his young, pregnant wife Miriam. They had taken a room on the first floor, at the front, the month before. He was a riveter of footwear, then in employment in George Street in Spitalfields, and she stayed at home, growing fatter, and doted on by her mother-in-law Dinah, who lived on nearby Grove Street, and whose house she would visit every morning to eat breakfast. On the evening of Monday 27 June, Isaac arrived home at nine o'clock, drank half a pint of beer for supper, and fell serenely asleep. Miriam wrote a letter to her father, went out to have it addressed – she wrote only in Yiddish, and Isaac not at all – and, returning home, retired for the night. The door to their room was locked, and the key was on the inside.

Isaac rose at six o'clock the next morning, chatting to an awakened Miriam and praying by the little table below the east-facing window. He left the house at a quarter past, unlocking the door to the room on his way out, but leaving the key on the inside, and the door itself closed, but not locked. Miriam remained in bed, wearing her chemise, the dawn tilting in under the blind.

Then followed the lost hours. At her house on Grove Street, Dinah Angel puzzled at her daughter-in-law's unusual failure to appear for breakfast – she was normally there by half past seven, or half past eight at the latest, and by eleven o'clock her wonder had turned to anxiety. She went to 16 Batty Street and found the landlady, Leah Lipski, in the kitchen.

'Have you seen anything of my daughter today?' asked Dinah.

'No,' replied Leah. 'You had better go up and see her.'

Dinah climbed the stairs to the first floor, and Leah heard her try the handle of the door to Miriam's room. 'Miriam,' called Dinah. There was no answer.

From the ground floor, Leah listened as Dinah struggled to attract Miriam's attention. 'You go up and help,' she suggested to another lodger, Mrs Levy, and Mrs Levy did, peering into the blackness of the keyhole in the bedroom door, in which the key stood, useless, on

Ropewalk Gardens, a miniaturized and renamed incarnation of Grove Street. (Author's collection)

The building which now stands on the site of 16 Batty Street. (Author's collection)

the inside, where Isaac had left it. Still there was no response from Miriam. Still the door seemed not to give.

Set part of the way up the staircase to the second floor was a small internal window looking into the Angels' room. Although it was covered by a curtain, this afforded little privacy: 'By putting your face close to the window,' explained Leah, later on, 'you can see through the muslin.' Mrs Levy squinted through the window, picking out Miriam's form, motionless and apparently swooning on the bed, through the ghost of the material. Leah had arrived on the landing – the growing misgivings of the ladies had been increasingly audible from the coffee-smelling kitchen – and, between the three of them, the alarmed women broke open the door.

Miriam was lying on her back with her head inclined slightly to the right, towards the wall. One arm was across her chest. From the corner of her mouth bubbled an ugly yellow froth, and her chemise was unevenly patterned, as if it had been somehow burnt in a constellation of countless separate spots. Leah grabbed one of Miriam's arms and shook her, desperate to see signs of life.

But Miriam was dead, and Leah ran down the stairs and into the street, racing for Dr John William Kay, who kept his surgery at 100 Commercial Road, on the north-eastern corner of Batty Street. Mrs Levy fled northwards, reaching George Street through the hot labyrinth of streets which knotted together to the north of the Whitechapel Road. There she alerted Isaac Angel to the sudden, grotesque demise of his spouse, and Angel hurried back to Batty Street, only to find himself stopped by the pity and sympathy of Miriam's

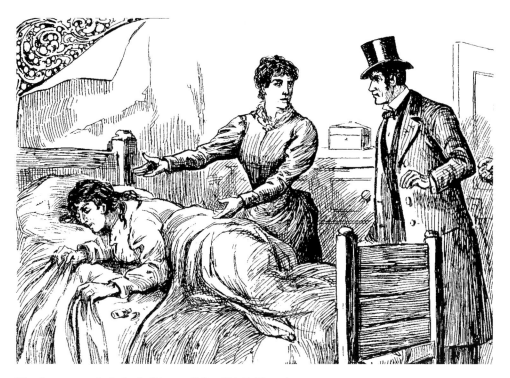

The doctor attends the body. (*Famous Crimes*, Vol. II, No. 14)

discoverers at the door to his little room – not until the Thursday, two days later, would he see her unhappy corpse.

★

Kay, the doctor, was not in, but Leah encountered his assistant, William Piper. He arrived at the house at half past eleven, and found the death room crowded with the curious, all gazing down at Miriam's remains. 'I felt that there had been foul play,' recalled Piper, coolly, and he cleared the room of its visitors and went to lock the door. The key was still in the lock, on the inside. Piper removed it, passed through the doorway onto the landing, and found that the door would not close. The bolt of the lock was shot, and, though he tried, Piper could not unlock it from the outside. He went back inside the room and turned the bolt from there. Set into the doorjamb, the box, which, under ordinary circumstances, received the bolt, seemed to Piper to be loose, and not deep enough. He passed back onto the landing, locked the door, kept the key, and went to fetch Kay.

John William Kay, who had received his license from the Society of Apothecaries in 1858, who had been a member of the Royal College of Surgeons since 1859, and who had graduated *Medicinæ Doctor* from the University of Giessen in 1872, was in his early fifties, a native of Huddersfield, and a widower of six years. In addition to his daily practice, he had trailed some of the East End's typically anomic cases through the grim courts for twenty years and more, giving his professional opinion on local offences actuated by the desperation, carelessness, drunkenness or, occasionally, vanity of their perpetrators. Through the Commercial Road and its dark tributaries an excited crowd now began to push its way as news of the strange death of Miriam Angel began to travel. The doctor, ahead of the mob, negotiated his way up the stairs and across the crowded first-floor landing of 16 Batty Street. William Piper, his assistant, produced the key to the room, turned the bolt in the lock, and opened the door.

Kay went to the unmoving Miriam. Plainly, she had been poisoned by the administration of a powerful acid. Yellow stains covered her hands, trickled from between her lips, were on her neck, her chest, her bedclothes. The almost celestial pattern on her chemise had been formed when, still conscious, she had coughed the poison back out. Kay opened her mouth, finding the palate horribly corroded; the tongue and throat were in a similar condition. The right eye was swollen and blackened, as if Miriam had been struck. Kay turned back the sheets – she lay naked from the waist down, and with her legs spread apart. Turning to the clutch of men who had anxiously followed him into the room, Kay suggested that they begin looking for a bottle. Nothing was to be done for poor Miriam.

Harris Dywien of Fairclough Street was a friend of the Angels, and had arrived at the house after hearing the screams of Leah Lipski, Mrs Levy and Dinah Angel. He scrabbled under the bed in search of clues, but found only some old clothes – and then, suddenly, a human hand.

'I think there is a body here,' said Dywien.

Kay pulled the bed away from the wall, and peered down into the space beyond. Angled back at him, there was a face, quite still, the eyes shut.

'Why, it is a man!' said Kay. He shook this second body, not knowing whether it was alive or dead, and the body did not respond. He slapped it on the face, and its eyes flickered open. Its pulse beat. Its mouth was the theatre of a miniature version of the damage which had been done to Miriam's; again, there was the same distinctive corrosion, but in this man, the damage was so slight, Kay thought, as to fail to account for his apparent unconsciousness. Kay put several questions to him – some in English, some in German – but the man made no reply, and Kay wondered at this, since the injuries to the man's throat were not, he thought, sufficient to cut off his speech. At Kay's request, the astonished Dywien ran for a policeman, and the strange, speechless man was lifted from his hiding place, glancing impassively at the dead woman on the bed, before being conveyed through the angry crowd outside the house to the police station on Leman Street.

Some time later, the crowd drifted away, but not before they had witnessed the removal of Miriam's remains, carried in a coffin on the silent shoulders of the undertaker's men. There were a thousand people there – perhaps two thousand – crammed into a street 26ft 9ins wide. One of them was Isaac Angel, caught in the helpless throes of grief, wringing his hands, gazing after the coffin, and moaning, in the words of one journalist, who charmlessly reflected the contemporary sentiment, 'My vife! My vife!'

★

From the police station, the man from the Angels' locked room was moved to the London Hospital, where he remained, the newspapers said, in a precarious condition. He had been identified as Israel Lipski, then occupying the top room of 16 Batty Street, but of no relation to his landlady – indeed, prior to his arrival in London in 1885 from Poland, his surname had been Lobulsk. Until 20 June 1887, a week and a day before Miriam Angel's death, he had worked for Mark Katz in Watney Court, making sticks for umbrellas, but he harboured dreams of self-employment – even the employment of others – and,

The St George in the East Mortuary, where Miriam Angel's remains were taken. (Author's collection)

The London Hospital, where Lipski stayed briefly after his non-fatal dose. (Author's collection)

despite his strapped circumstances, elected to set himself up in competition to Katz. He secured the services of a rather immature boy named Richard Pittman – quite the sort of innocent to merrily attach himself to the unrealistic reveries of another – and sent Pittman on an expensive spree through the hardware shops of Whitechapel, buying provisions for the new business. Lipski's room in Batty Street would serve as factory as well as home, although this added a premium to his rent. The enterprise was already a costly one, and the work had not yet begun.

Simon Rosenbloom, too, had been approached to throw in his lot with Lipski's grand scheme. He, like Lipski, had apparently tired of working for Mark Katz, and agreed to turn up at 16 Batty Street at seven o'clock on the morning of the fatal Tuesday. When he did, he found Lipski restless, dashing out for a second vice in order to kickstart their work, and returning without one, grumbling that the shop had not yet opened. Another itinerant worker, Isaac Schmuss, appeared during Lipski's next absence – he was gone from his little factory-room at a little after eight, *prima facie* in search of the new vice and a sponge for Pittman – but Schmuss did not stay long, having rapidly formed the opinion that Lipski's promises of work seemed unlikely to materialise. Then Rosenbloom heard the screaming, and went down to Miriam Angel's room, going in while William Piper was there, and going in again when Dr Kay arrived.

Against this, the ailing Lipski made his own very different statement. In his version, coaxed out of him at the hospital on the evening of the crime, his largesse remained unaffected by his previous spending: he cast sovereigns around for brandy, and offered work with almost frivolous abandon to men whom he scarcely knew. Rosenbloom and Schmuss, he said, had ambushed him on the first-floor landing as he was coming upstairs from the yard, demanding money from him, and Lipski's visions of success in business faded as they tipped acid down his throat. They had already killed Miriam, and threw Lipski under her bed, where he lay, waiting for death. As it happened, Dr Kay had tested the substance which had accounted for Miriam, and which had injured Lipski, identifying it as nitric acid. In Backchurch Lane, Charles Moore, the manager of an oil shop, recalled selling an ounce of *aqua fortis* – dilute nitric acid – to Lipski on the morning in question. He had warned Lipski that the substance was poisonous.

Lipski's rendition of the events of the fateful day seemed at variance with the ascertainable facts. He had bought the acid, and had it on his body and his clothes – Rosenbloom and Schmuss were unmarked by it, and, even if Lipski had indeed subsided weakly in the face of his new employees' unlikely blitz, Miriam had not. Her hair was found dishevelled about the pillow, and, prior to the blow to the head which stunned her, she must have seen, and struggled with, her attacker. On his wrists and forearms, Lipski bore scratches, as if inflicted upon him by another individual acting in self-defence. Lipski made no remark about the matter of the door to the room being found locked, with him on the inside, and Rosenbloom and Schmuss demonstrably on the outside. Locked-room puzzles are beloved of the crime fiction writer, but they typically demand the absence of the murderer – here, Lipski remained in the locked room, which rather undermined the expected element of mystery. He was promptly charged with the murder of Miriam Angel, despite his statement, and identified as the likely perpetrator by a coroner's jury. The case was delivered to the Old Bailey, to be heard in sessions commencing on Friday 29 July 1887, scarcely a month after Miriam's death.

★

The courtroom had its own strange pharmacopeia. On the bench sat the opium-smoking judge, Mr Justice James Fitzjames Stephen, whose mind had begun to stray as a result of a stroke he had suffered a couple of years previously. For the defence, iridescent within legal circles but inactive and quite possibly incapable of making any serious contribution to Lipski's cause, there appeared Gerald Geoghegan, an Irish barrister apparently notable for his frequent bouts of heavy drinking. Geoghegan's renowned advocacy would easily have bettered that of his senior at the trial, Aeneas McIntyre, but this uncelebrated gentleman, a civil court lawyer unused to the criminal stage, was, *de facto*, all that stood between Lipski and the gallows. Geoghegan, though retained by the solicitor for the defence, sat through the proceedings without stirring in Lipski's aid, and perhaps in the claws of one of his spasms of alcoholism. This sort of erratic behaviour may have affected his practice until his death, by a supposedly accidental overdose, in 1902.

In the dock stood the alleged poisoner, the third part of this chemical trinity. For two days, witnesses filed through the court, probed first by the esteemed pairing of Harry Poland and Charles Mathews, senior-ranking barristers to the Treasury, and then cross-examined by the insipid McIntyre. Much of the evidence was interpreted – neither Rosenbloom nor Schmuss, for example, Lipski's own suspects, could speak English, and the questions asked of them by counsel, crucial to the jury's understanding of Lipski's defence, were framed in English, moulded into Yiddish, answered in Yiddish, and delivered back to the court in English. This must have rendered the process disjointed, and it was similarly pointed out, in retrospect, that the mainly Yiddish-speaking Lipski's access to the evidence of those witnesses who spoke only in English must have been limited. Lipski's recovery from the effects of his poisoning had been entire, but, in the circumstances, he can only have found the trial as a whole confusing, and some parts of it incomprehensible.

The court's attention was occupied for hours in elucidating the obscure choreography of the chaotic ballet surrounding the key, the lock, and the bottle – this latter item having been located in the room by Harris Dywien, and identified by Charles Moore as the one which Lipski had brought to him to be filled with acid, but also seen in the hand of Rosenbloom at or around the time of Lipski's discovery under the bed. Here, the jigsaw pieces of individual memories competed with one another, and, sometimes, testimony which seemed destined to lead towards a conclusion retreated suddenly into entropy. William Piper was sure that the bolt of the lock had been shot, and, of course, Mrs Levy *et al* had failed to get the door open without a certain degree of force; but was there another way in which the door could have been locked from the inside by a murderer standing on the outside? Leah Lipski described a hole in the Angels' door, big enough to fit three fingers in, through which she could touch the key when the key was on the inside, but without being able to gain the leverage to turn it in the lock. Schmuss, meanwhile, was, as he readily acknowledged, a locksmith by trade; but there was no proof, despite Lipski's allegations, that Schmuss's dexterity and professional expertise had assisted him in committing the crime. McIntyre's unconvincing questioning steered Lipski's defence, stumbling, haphazard, towards the hazy concept of a reasonable doubt – this, of course, was all that was necessary for the acquittal of the defendant – but, at the close of the second day, Lipski's guilt was ascertained by the jury after just eight minutes' deliberation. Out of court at seventeen minutes to five, they were back at nine minutes before the hour. Mr Justice Stephen donned the black cap and sentenced Israel Lipski to death. Asked whether he had anything to say, Lipski remarked, 'I am innocent; I did not do it.'

The controversy of the verdict splashed across the media. Lipski's story seemed unlikely, but still problems remained. In court, Leah Lipski (who had declined to testify via an interpreter) had pronounced herself uncertain that the door had been locked, *contra* the recollections of Piper; and the acquisition of an ounce of *aqua fortis* seemed insufficient to account for the degree of damage done to Miriam and Lipski himself – the existence of a second ounce was postulated, and there was no evidence to suggest where this extra acid had been procured. Lipski's effigy had appeared in Madame Tussaud's waxworks within a week of the trial, but doubts about his authorship of the crime of which he had been convicted grew more and more voluble. Leading the objections was W.T. Stead, the editor of the *Pall Mall Gazette*, and an indefatigable gadfly jangling the nerves of the government. Stead was a complex character, an inscrutable amalgam of bitter prejudices and deeply-felt compassions, then bristling at the paradox of the appointment of the Catholic Henry Mathews to the position of Home Secretary in a pro-Union administration. Lipski's case offered another means by which to irritate the establishment, and, day after day, Stead filled

Israel Lipski. (The National Archives, ref. COPY 1/381/266)

his pages with rhetoric, loudly arguing for the release of Lipski, the victim, he said, of a gross miscarriage of justice.

Mr Justice Stephen reflected gloomily upon his summing-up, writing frequently to the Home Office, and poring over newspaper reports of the trial. In a case which, in many ways, defied easy understanding, the prosecution had fought shy of ascribing to Lipski a motive for his offence. Apparently energised by his new business venture, and engaged, as it happened, to be married to a young lady by the name of Kate Lyons, Lipski hardly seemed to be the kind of character to cast his future to the wind for the sake of – what? – impromptu, non-consensual sex with Miriam Angel? This seemed difficult to sustain. Miriam had been discovered with her legs apart and her lower half exposed, and Dr Kay had found a substance resembling semen in her vagina, but microscopic examination had shown that, whatever it was, there were no spermatozoa within it. If not sex, then, this left only the motive of money; but the Angels had no money, and common sense suggested that thieves typically fled the scene with their loot, and did not normally lie down to die under somebody else's bed on commission of their act. Stephen, in his charge to the jury, had been less circumspect, and began to feel that he had pushed the jury too firmly towards a decision regarding the motive of the killer. If they believed the motive was sexual, he said, the situation argued for a solitary culprit; he, personally, found this explanation 'more probable' than its pecuniary alternative. This comment he now came to regret.

With Stead fanning the flames of public feeling, the Home Office looked again and again at the evidence of Lipski's guilt. Once, his execution was deferred to accommodate further enquiries – the lock was examined and re-examined, the acid tested and re-tested, and discovered, in fact, to be a mixture consisting of three-fifths sulphuric acid to two-fifths nitric acid, matching the ratios found in a sample of Charles Moore's stock. But still the web of circumstantial evidence stayed half-closed, half-open: nobody except Moore had ever seen Lipski with the bottle in which he had, it appeared, kept his acid, prior to its unhappy use. Stephen wrote glumly to his wife, describing the delay, the continual meetings with political and legal luminaries, and the gnawing doubt about the justice of Lipski's conviction as 'painful'. Renegade information reached the authorities' ears which sketched out a previous relationship between the victim and her killer, conducted in Poland and broken off, perhaps, by Miriam herself. This suggested a third motive – revenge – but, predictably, the idea turned out to be a romantic fancy, empty of substance. The hours ticked agonisingly by: Lipski would be hanged on Monday 22 August 1887, unless the Home Secretary, who sat with the judge, both silent in thought, into the night of the Sunday before the execution, could find reliable grounds on which to overturn the court's decision, and recommend a commutation.

★

Then came the knock at the door, and the *deus ex machina* of the prison messenger. With hours left in the condemned cell in Newgate, the prisoner had disclosed his awful method, and the fact that his description of events jarred with the much-pored-over evidence appears to have eluded the authorities in their marred elation. Dr Kay, examining the body post-mortem, had estimated that Miriam's death had occurred at about half past eight in the morning, roughly the latest time at which she would normally go to her mother-in-law's house for breakfast. Lipski himself suggested that the death had taken place 'only a very short time' before his discovery under the bed. But what could have detained Miriam that morning, such that she remained in bed, alive and apparently well, at, say, ten or even eleven o'clock? There was no explanation for the anomaly which Lipski imputed to her routine. Lipski described theft as his motive for entering the room, but why would he have locked the door behind him, as he also claimed to have done? This could only have hindered his escape, supposing that he had needed to make one. He complained of having felt 'tired' of life, and said that he had bought the acid from Moore with the intention of committing suicide, but this conflicted with the apparent optimism of his recent business activity. And if one did feel like committing suicide, and if one was armed with the tools to do it, why would one bother undertaking a pointless theft from the room of an obviously poor couple? It was hardly a means to his own identified end, but objections to Lipski's guilt now seemed to evaporate into nothing, and, as night became day, Newgate prepared for a hanging.

★

The rumour of Lipski's having cheated even the hangman spread after his death. Supposedly, he had died of fright on his way to the scaffold, but this seemed like wishful thinking on the part of the living, who were, no doubt, desperate to attach a romantic dénouement to the story. Likewise, the awkward confession seemed like wishful thinking on the part of Lipski. The financial motive stood up only to perfunctory examination – Lipski was indeed short of money, and had tried to borrow some from his landlady, without success, on the morning of the murder, but the brutality of the crime, and the position in which Miriam Angel was discovered lying on the bed, made rape a more probable motive. We have no way of knowing whether Lipski was able to produce sperm, or, more precisely, whether Lipski's semen contained sperm, and if it did not, then the substance in Miriam's vagina may very well have been an overlooked clue to the events of the fateful morning. To this extent, Mr Justice Stephen might have been correct in his analysis of what had happened at Batty Street, although he was probably incorrect to mention it in court.

However, the reader may be forgiven for finding even this conclusion unsatisfactory. How abhorrently suddenly must the urge to rape and kill Miriam Angel have seized Israel Lipski? Can he have been an apparently hopeful stick-maker one moment, a man engaged to be married, a man known to have been of good character to those who lived closest to him; and then, almost instantly, can he have abandoned himself to the futility of capital crime? Only the purchase of the acid seems to hint at the existence of Lipski's darker side prior to his crossing the threshold into the Angels' room – in his choice of coolly shop-bought weapon, there may have been an element of planning, although the psychological machinery which drives a man to poison a woman with whom he has no known connection remains inevitably obscure. From his photograph, Lipski appears well-presented, thoughtful, even gentle. Under the surface, though, who can tell?

Three

1888

In the first hours of 31 August 1888, Whitechapel's Year Zero, the sky to the south glowed red. At the Shadwell Dry Dock, flames licked from the rigging of a doomed ship to hundreds of tons of coal, stored nearby. The scene attracted a crowd, and the fire's luminous effects were visible from higher ground miles off.

Meanwhile, back in Whitechapel, two labourers on their way to work had happened upon a woman's body lying supine and quite still in Buck's Row, just behind the Whitechapel Road. Initially, one of them – giving his name as Charles Cross – had mistaken her for an unwanted tarpaulin – now, in the shadows of the narrow street, it was difficult to tell whether she was drunk, or dead. Only when PC John Neil arrived to shine his lantern on the unmoving form did anyone notice the awful laceration across her throat; and it was not until the body was taken to the mortuary that the deep cuts to the abdomen were found. Through the worst of them, the intestines protruded, tempted to uncoil by the knife which had ripped through the layers of flesh above them.

So ended a life, and presently it became apparent that the body was that of one Mary Ann Nichols. Alcoholic, destitute, deserted by her husband, and on distant terms with her children, Nichols had arrived in the East End only a few months before, after a spell in domestic service had ended rather badly. Nichols's erstwhile employers' ardent teetotalism had failed to impress her, and, on the last night of her life, she had squandered her doss money, normally fourpence for an uncomfortable bed in a common lodging house on Thrawl Street, a few times over. Drunk, dispossessed, and relying on prostitution to bring in the pennies, she had been seen staggering at the junction of Osborn Street and Whitechapel Road hours earlier, determined despite her indisposition to find another customer, and either to top up with drink, or to take shelter from the night's *son et lumière* storms in the cheerless sanctuary of her dosshouse.

★

A body being wheeled into the morgue. Jack the Ripper's victims would have been brought in on a cart like this one.

The terracotta sign of the Frying Pan, where Mary Ann Nichols squandered her money on the night of her death. (Author's collection)

The next day, Nichols's dispassionate, apparently meaningless murder stimulated the local imaginations. It was, the streets said, the coming of a monster, perhaps one related by bastard blood to the beast ominously foreseen by the socialist visionaries. In their apocalyptic moments, they had told of a great, uncontrollable power emerging from the slums – this was meant as a political analogy, but, in the wake of the murder, the analogy now seemed immature and near-sighted. An *eminence gris* had arrived in the East End, and he held life and death in his grip, was capable of swift and sure action, and left no obvious clue to his daytime identity. This last feature of the Buck's Row crime – the sheer anonymity of it all – thrilled and terrified the masses, and, in the anxious clamour for justice, it took little time for the public's attention to attach itself to a possible offender: the pseudonymous Leather Apron, believed to be identical with John Pizer, a man reputedly in the habit of abusing prostitutes, and a convenient focus for the widespread distress. But, before the police could find Pizer, who appeared to have gone to ground, the killer struck again.

★

This time, the victim was Annie Chapman. Like Nichols, she scratched a living through prostitution, balancing her income against the nightly expenses of shelter and drink. Better times had passed her by and, as she left her common lodging house on Dorset Street, penniless and vowing to earn her keep, in the early hours of 8 September, she was nearing fifty, shabby, malnourished, bruised from a recent fight, and dying, anyway, of a disease affecting the lungs and the brain.

Chapman's corpse was discovered shortly after sunrise, lying by the back steps of the congested dwelling-house at 29 Hanbury Street. A shared passageway gave access from the street to the back yard – the doors leading off the corridor, and those on the storeys above, reached via the stairs, all led to separate rooms which, at that time, seventeen people called home. Running the risk of interruption at any moment, the murderer had taken Chapman through the house to the back yard, strangled her (her tongue was left poking between her teeth, a clear sign of asphyxiation), lowered her to the ground, cut her throat; and then he sliced away at her body, opening her like a treasure chest and revelling in what he found within. He drew out her intestines and looped them over her shoulder, though they were still attached by a sinew to the abdominal cavity; he removed her uterus, two-thirds of her bladder, and the upper part of her vagina; the off-cuts of the belly wall he discarded, and left them lying in pools of blood. This was an extension of the violent death of Nichols, with the lacerations to her abdomen amplified into the para-surgical explorations of Chapman's viscera. The excision of the organs from Chapman's body (another point of departure, and a horrifying new development in the psychology of the East End murderer) was performed swiftly and, some thought, expertly. The doctor who examined Chapman's remains suspected that the killer was anatomically informed. Miraculously, the whole thing was achieved without disturbing the slumbers of any of the residents of the house.

This latest crime brought crowds to the doorway of 29 Hanbury Street, and their demands for the apprehension of Leather Apron moved towards a shrill crescendo. Pizer was arrested on 10 September, dragged off to Leman Street police station by Sergeant

Osborn Street, Whitechapel.

Dorset Street, Spitalfields.

The Princess Alice, supposedly John Pizer's favourite pub. (Author's collection)

William Thick, and capably proved his innocence when he was found to have been in Holloway on the night of Nichols's murder, remarking on the fire-tinted sky to a policeman on the Seven Sisters Road. He had been lying low since returning to the East End after his brother had warned him about the intensity of local feeling against that man of mystery, Leather Apron – Pizer expressed wonder that he had ever been known by that sobriquet, and his family and acquaintances did too, but, clearly, he had erred on the side of caution, and kept clear of a passionate, vengeful mob.

The newspapers exploited the terror which now gripped Whitechapel, following the invisible footsteps of the invisible killer through the gossip and rumours of the grim maze of streets. With belief in the guilt of Leather Apron dissolving, public suspicions scattered themselves increasingly widely, and the perfect vision of retrospect imparted significance to incidents which might once – had they occurred the previous year, for example – have been considered mundane, or at most merely curious. One of the most promising of a dismal bunch seemed to be Mrs Fiddymont's report of a bloodstained man stopping for half a pint of beer at her public house in Brushfield Street, and this on the very morning of Annie Chapman's death. The man's behaviour seemed suspicious, and Mrs Fiddymont pointed him out to a friend; to modern minds turned cynical to the well-meaning naïveté of the East End's then-panicked residents, the idea of the murderer stopping for refreshment, covered in gore, in a public house perhaps two and a half minutes' walk from the scene of his most recent outrage may appear deeply unconvincing. The police took Mrs Fiddymont seriously, but she may have seen a man named Isenschmidt, and he was mad, but not the murderer.

For three weeks after the murder of Chapman, Whitechapel awoke each morning to find its streets unstained by fresh blood. The killer was quiet, and the fearful anticipation of his next crime increased in strict proportion to his present inactivity. There remained no clues to his whereabouts, let alone his name, and while policemen were poured onto the streets by their helpless superiors, and private citizens banded together in vigilance – not far from vigilante – gangs, the Whitechapel murderer disdained to find further work for his idle, bloodied hands. September was nearly out before he condescended to strike again.

A Ripper tour at
the site of Annie
Chapman's murder.
(Author's collection)

Gardiner's Corner,
at the junction of
Whitechapel High
Street and Leman
Street.

Brushfield Street;
the Fruit and Wool
Exchange stands over
the site of Millers
Court. (Author's
collection)

★

Elizabeth Gustafsdotter had arrived in England from Sweden in the 1860s, a registered prostitute in her home country, the mother of a stillborn child, a victim of venereal diseases and, perhaps, seduced by the public image of London as a centre of commerce and prosperity. It would be some time before concerted and popular efforts to remediate the desperate conditions in Whitechapel and other, similar, slum areas would be made, and, until they were, it was distinctly possible not only for those from overseas, but also for British newspaper readers from the middle classes and above, to remain oblivious of the real state of things in the East End. Elizabeth herself can hardly have remained ignorant of the truth of social disadvantage in Victorian London for very long – little better off in England than she had been in Gothenburg, she married a man named John Stride in the parish church of St Giles in the Fields, in Soho, in 1869, and this was a very poor area, long marked by poverty, crime, and disease. With social opportunities at a premium, and with temptation and desperation always liable to find a way to make things worse, Stride descended through the usual levels of social displacement, moving east through the workhouses and dosshouses, through drink and despair, until, by 29 September 1888, she was reduced to shamming affection with a man sheltering in the doorway of the Bricklayers' Arms, on Settles Street, hoping that he had the money for gin, beer, or sex.

She turned up in Dutfield's Yard, off Berner Street, two hours later, in the early morning of 30 September, when a pony belonging to one Louis Diemschitz refused to move past a heap lying in the impenetrable shadows. Diemschitz struck a match, peered at the

Casuals waiting for admission to a London workhouse. Many of the Ripper's victims had been in and out of these institutions for years; some of the clothing Polly Nichols was wearing on the night she died, for example, came from Lambeth Workhouse.

recumbent form through the dim haze of the flame, and feared that he had discovered his wife in a drunken swoon. He went to summon assistance from his acquaintances inside the International Workingmen's Educational Club, the southern wall of which formed the northern boundary of the narrow, sightless yard, and they returned to find Stride dead, her throat cut, but her abdomen not mutilated. If this was the killer of Nichols and Chapman, the terrible pattern of worsening violence against the corpse which seemed to have been developing was suddenly abandoned, but the idea that Diemschitz had interrupted the murderer in mid-flow quickly gained currency. Had there been someone hiding in the shadows, so viscous was the darkness in Dutfield's Yard, Diemschitz need not have seen him.

The East End crowded with police officers, doctors, and the traumatised public, all desperate for the most recent news, or any hint of the perpetrator's identity, but the murderer, according to his legend, went west, up the Commercial Road to Mitre Square, and coolly murdered Catherine Eddowes, destroying her with the casual brutality he had – again, according to the legend – been unable to deploy in his interrupted attack on Elizabeth Stride. This murder brought the City of London Police – a fiercely independent outfit, unallied to the Metropolitan Police – into the affair, and now both forces pursued this unseen, faceless killer. After the murder of Eddowes, he left perhaps his only clue, dropping a piece of her apron, marked with blood and excrement as if the blade of a knife had been drawn across it, in a doorway in Goulston Street. Above it was written a short indictment of the vast local Jewish population, although its spelling and grammar were such as to make its real meaning difficult to divine. It seems more likely that the anti-Semitic message had some tangible, proximal meaning to its author – who was, perhaps, a gentile in dispute with a Jewish trader – than that it possessed any significance to the murders and their associated panic. Of course, the killer was unflappable, but it seems impossible to prove that he was in any way linked with the graffito, and, if he was the murderer of Stride, he must have known that his activities would already have caused the area to flood with police officers. To stop and record his feelings about his Jewish neighbours in chalk on a convenient doorjamb stretches even the most confident criminal's *sangfroid* to unlikely lengths.

The murder of Eddowes was the most hideous to date. She had been made a plaything for the killer's most remote whims, bearing apparently functionless wounds to the face and, via the vast schism which the murderer had opened in Eddowes's body, stabs and cuts to the liver. Another stab had fallen in the groin. From the abdomen, the intestines had once again been lifted out and placed above the shoulder, and this time a separate length of about 2ft had been cut away and placed, for whatever reason, between the trunk and the left arm. The left kidney was missing entirely, leaving a drooping length of renal artery behind, and most of the uterus was gone. The whole scene was one of intricate horror, and difficult to interpret – nicks and cuts here and there, such as the one removing the skin at the end of the nose, spoke of decadence and indulgence on the part of the perpetrator, unless they were nothing more than slips of the knife. As had been the case with Chapman, the anatomical and surgical expertise of the murderer were pondered – one school of thought held that the removal of the kidney, in the dark and in a hurry, would have required skill and precision, and this, in theory, reduced the probability of Eddowes's incidental wounds being caused by fumbling hands; but the doctor who examined the body post-mortem felt that a mental map of the internal organs might have served the murderer well enough to perform his operation, and that formal medical experience would have been unnecessary. In these circumstances, some of the assorted wounds left decorating the desperate corpse might have been considered accidental. Enquiries of this sort, sourcing evidence from those who could reasonably be called experts, were testimony to the thorough medico-legal approach then developing in the coroners' courts: every detail of Eddowes's mutilation was described and defined, with the jury reaching the unfortunately inevitable conclusion that the murder had been committed by a person – or persons – unknown.

★

The literate public, for whom press coverage of the murders was bringing blurry old Whitechapel suddenly and startlingly into focus, now haemorrhaged letters. Some were pleas for social reform, blaming the murders on a general moral degradation which, they felt, went hand-in-hand with material want; some suggested solutions, identifying the murderer, or nudged the police towards redoubled efforts to locate him; but many claimed to be from the killer himself. The most famous of these were sent not to the police, but to the newspapers, and by this oddly democratic method was the name Jack the Ripper created, an identity, suitably mysterious and yet chillingly familiar, which seemed to encapsulate the mundane terror inflicted upon his society by one driven individual. However, even these letters – which purported to carry important clues, as the killer tormented his frustrated pursuers – shed their evidential value as doubts about their authenticity multiplied. The balance of them are interesting only to the extent that they capture the Victorian public in a spate of nervous excitement, their gruesome imaginations running away with them in their eager correspondence.

For another month, Jack the Ripper rested, allowing the story of the so-called Double Event to unravel: remarkably, the murders of Stride and Eddowes had been separated by no more than an hour. Witnesses shuffled through the inquest proceedings, providing inadequate testimony, and painting a picture of the East End in which few were above suspicion, and violence was smeared endemically through the community. On the night of the double murder, both victims had been spotted with men who might, perhaps, have been the Ripper, if only they could be identified. In Stride's case, a fearful Jewish resident, Israel Schwartz, saw her shoved into the pitch darkness of Dutfield's Yard, and felt that he himself was chased away as a potential witness to something, but there was no way of knowing who the generic bullies of the East End – all moustaches and broad shoulders, according to the coroner's enquiries – might really have been. With the notable professional exception of doctors, who carried the black Gladstone bag of Ripper legend and fell under public suspicion whenever they did, the alarming truth facing the frightened people of Whitechapel was that the Ripper was probably one of them, indistinguishable from the majority.

The last murder occurred on 9 November, when the Ripper broke his abstinence by obliterating Mary Jane Kelly in her tiny rented room in Millers Court, off Dorset Street. It was the only Ripper murder to take place inside a building, and the killer gave full vent to his instincts, apparently secure in the understanding that he would not be interrupted.

Typical customers at one of Whitechapel's many public houses, *c.* 1900.

The catalogue of the dissection makes for depressing reading: among other injuries, including what were probably defence wounds to her hands and forearms, Kelly had had her nose, cheeks, eyebrows and ears partially removed, her breasts cut off, the muscles between her ribs scored, her abdomen opened, her left thigh denuded of flesh to the bone. She had been emptied to a greater extent than any of her predecessors: her uterus, one kidney and one breast were left under her head; the second breast was by her right foot; her liver lay between her feet; her intestines were at her right side and her spleen at her left; on a table near the bed lay heaps of soft tissue, removed from the abdomen and thighs. The chest was open, and the heart taken from its surroundings, and nowhere to be found.

The anonymity of the Ripper's victims – the analogue of his own invisibility – was epitomised in Kelly. Dehumanised by her murderer in death, she had actively depersonalised herself in life by providing her most recent beau, Joseph Barnett, with a vague, cautious account of her life, none of which seems to tally with the historical record. The stories of a dead husband – a man named Davies, blown up in a mine explosion – and of an 1884 excursion to France as the courtesan of a rich gentleman, encountered while she was working in a high-class, West End brothel, ultimately fail to convince. In truth, she was one displaced black sheep among the crowds who herded into the East End, reinventing themselves on the way. Many of the Ripper's victims had tales to tell, and not all of them were founded in reality: Elizabeth Stride claimed to have lost her husband and some of her children in the sinking of the *Princess Alice* on the Thames in 1878, and she described the heel of a man's boot smashing her hard palate in the struggle for survival, but the autopsy found no sign of any such injury. Whitechapel was a playground for the unrepentant fantasist, with many of its residents linked in mutual delusion. No family attended Mary Jane Kelly's funeral; such was the smokescreen behind which she lived out her last years.

The death of Kelly in Millers Court was the worst exhibition of carnage yet, outstripping that of Eddowes, but most observers felt that the Ripper crimes ceased with her murder. This time, the Ripper really did rest, and other, subsequent Whitechapel murders (that of Alice Mackenzie in 1889, and that of Frances Coles in 1891) lacked the trademark violence of the original sequence. Whitechapel was relieved, and not simply because Jack the Ripper had desisted from his grim rampage: the killings had the secondary, and unintended, effect of increasing the public appetite for changes to the social machinery of the East End, and some measures of social welfare gradually improved over subsequent years as philanthropists, charities and the government began to invest in the area. Even this was relative, however, and poverty continued to animate many of Whitechapel's residents for years to come.

In spite of the popular relief, the Ripper's cessation demanded interpretation, and so began the scrap for the murderer's true identity, with suspicions predicated to a greater or (where this was convenient) a lesser extent on the extremely limited evidence he left behind him.

Some suspects, inevitably, were stronger than others. In 1894, an internal Scotland Yard communiqué named three individuals who were considered better candidates than one Thomas Cutbush, who had recently come to police attention after having exhibited a penchant for stabbing women from behind. This was the Macnaghten Memorandum, named after its author, a senior policeman, and one of the key texts in Ripper suspect history.

The first of Macnaghten's suspects, and to his mind the best, was Montague John Druitt, who had drowned himself in the Thames less than a month after Kelly's murder – perhaps, Macnaghten thought, because the slaughterhouse scene in Millers Court had driven him to insanity and suicide. Against Druitt ranged the suggestions that he was 'sexually insane' and had medical expertise – in fact, he was probably a homosexual, rather than a sexual mutilator of female prostitutes; and he was a lawyer and a teacher, not a doctor. Druitt's apogee as a Ripper candidate occurred in the 1960s, since which time his star has faded, and, examined critically, and with due regard to the contemporary suspicion of him, the case against him seems weak. That Druitt was an individual with a sad story to tell remains likely, but he was probably not the scourge of Whitechapel.

While Druitt exemplified the doctor-stereotype which had coalesced around Jack the Ripper, Aaron Kosminski, Macnaghten's second suspect, stood for the figure of the murderous Jew hinted at in the Goulston Street Graffito. Kosminski certainly courted trouble with the police – but, as it turned out, only for walking an unmuzzled dog, and, even then, not until after the sequence of murders had ended. This was hardly the defiant act of a daring, fearless killer. Finally, it is true, Kosminski departed from reality and was put into an asylum – Macnaghten described this as the fruit of an enduring addiction to masturbation, then considered a habit liable to induce madness. But Kosminski was, at heart, a docile soul who lived on until 1919 without betraying the violent impulses which must have driven Jack the Ripper. As far as anyone knows, none of the tangible evidence in the case pointed the finger at a Jewish maniac, and the so-called Polish Jew theory itself –

Sir Melville Macnaghten, the author of the
eponymous Memorandum.

endorsed elsewhere in Scotland Yard and, in recent commentaries, made to refer not only
to Kosminski but also to the apparently shadowy figures of Nathan Kaminsky and David
Cohen – smacks of an irrational, gentile terror, and the fear of invasion from the outside. In
his unlikely way, then, Aaron Kosminski may just have been a prototype Dracula, thirsting
for the blood of England's most vulnerable women. Bram Stoker's novel, crystallising this
anxiety, would follow before the end of the decade.

The third of Macnaghten's suspects, Michael Ostrog, was meant to have been a mad
Russian doctor, neatly bridging the gap between Druitt (the supposed clinician) and
Kosminski (the foreigner). Ostrog was a rogue, perhaps unpleasant company, but devoted
to theft and confidence trickery, sometimes executed under the alias of Count Sobieski,
the son of the exiled King of Poland. Among his other adventures, he was chased across
Woolwich Common by a group of cadets after stealing a metal tankard from the military
barracks, an escapade he explained in court by claiming to have been unsettled by sunstroke
and in the midst of a vivid race-running fantasy happily realised when the cadets made
their pursuit of him. Ostrog had difficulties maintaining his grip on sanity – or, at least,
he made some plausible approximations of lunacy – and remained fixed on apparently
silly thefts for years after the Ripper affair: in 1900, he was indeed in Whitechapel, but, far
from returning to his regime of terror of twelve years before, he merely stole a microscope
from the London Hospital. He is a fascinating individual, eccentric, and the product of his
own eccentric times, but Ostrog's credentials as Jack the Ripper are unconvincing: recent
research suggests that he was imprisoned in France at the relevant times, anyway.

Since Macnaghten, hundreds of further attempts to elucidate the identity of Jack the
Ripper have been made, and almost all of them have stumbled on the lack of evidence
tying any individual suspect to the crimes. History demands a greater weight of proof now
than once it did, but there can be little excuse for some of the more curious inventions of
authors of the past – for instance, the dangerous Russian, Pedachenko, who was the suspect

of 1950s theorist Donald McCormick, seems never to have actually existed. Whichever way one looks at it, this fact seriously affects the probability of his having been the killer. More recently, authors have been generally careful to avoid suspects who are purely imaginary, but this trend has given way to an over-abundance of celebrity suspects, most famously Prince Albert Victor, the effete grandson of Queen Victoria, but also including Lewis Carroll, Gladstone, Dr Barnardo, and Leopold II, King of the Belgians, who was apparently corrupted by gruesome scenes witnessed in the Congo and who decided to re-enact them in London in 1888. All of these people really existed – which stands to their advocates' advantage – but this hardly makes any one of them Jack the Ripper. A post-Freudian reliance on amateur psychology has also crept into Ripperology, offering a *carte blanche* to anyone prepared to guess at the way the killer's brain may have worked; and if it was not the gore of the Congo which affected the King of the Belgians, then perhaps it was some unspecified childhood trauma which Charles Dodgson – later Lewis Carroll, the author of the Alice books – later exorcised through the unlikely media of serial murder and clever anagrams. With the ground here obviously fecund, it is unlikely that the wellspring of new suspects will run dry in the near future.

★

The alarm which overtook the East End in 1888 had begun before the murder of Mary Ann Nichols. In April, Emma Elizabeth Smith had been attacked by a gang lurking in the shadows at the corner of Wentworth Street and Osborn Street – or so she said – and died from the internal injuries they caused her. Then, in early August, Martha Tabram died on a landing in George Yard Buildings, stabbed thirty-nine times, although *sans* the incisions which would characterise the Ripper's work. A man named John Saunders Reeves stumbled over her body, pooled in its own blood, prostrate in the early morning light, and a doctor was summoned to certify the death and to perform the post-mortem. This was Timothy Robert Killeen, then in practice at 68 Brick Lane, but probably an Irishman by birth, probably from a quiet and rural area, and very likely Catholic.

Tabram's vicious death – a kind of summation of East End depravity, which Killeen sharply juxtaposed with his gentle Irish home – forced the doctor's mind over the edge. Traumatised and rendered psychotic, he found himself *mirroring* the likely psychological trajectory of Tabram's killer, had he been serially inclined; involuntarily, Killeen had 'become' the killer, adopting his mentality and, by the end of August, taking his own first victim, Mary Ann Nichols.

The injuries to Nichols's abdomen, in their turn, began to express Killeen's own Catholic anxieties about female sexuality (advertised all around him in Whitechapel's legions of prostitutes); eight days later, the expert excision of Chapman's organs went a little further, and, with this murder, Killeen was practically on his own doorstep, only a little north and west of his home. Perhaps, in what remained of his conscience, the rapid intensification of Killeen's compulsive behaviour had begun to worry him at this point, for, like Dr Jekyll in the then-popular novel, he seems consciously to have attempted to contain his criminal inclinations, resulting in the quiet of the weeks in the second half of September. This, however, lasted only until his unconscious drives regained their inevitable superiority, and,

Above: Gunthorpe Street, once George Yard, and still with some of its late Victorian atmosphere. (Author's collection)

Left: Dr Killeen's Brick Lane residence, as it appears today. (Author's collection)

after the murder of Stride had been interrupted by Louis Diemschitz's pony, the crazed doctor displaced his pent-up anger against Eddowes, fleeing back in the direction of his surgery, and dropping the remnant of her apron in Goulston Street as he did so.

Through October, Killeen again attempted to exert control over his sudden proclivities, but with Mary Jane Kelly, he finally gave in to the full range of sexual and para-sexual influences which had spewed from his unconscious mind, vandalising her body horribly. Only by the theft of her heart – perhaps an instinctive or opportunistic act – was Killeen released from the grip of his psychosis: one of the wounds to Tabram's pin-cushion body had been directed through the heart, and this wound in itself (even in the absence of the thirty-eight other injuries) Killeen had considered sufficient to cause death. With the poetic removal of Kelly's heart, Killeen closed the circle of his ordeal, achieving life from the midst of death, but he realised that the East End remained on the alert for the killer, and that he could hardly expect to justify his sojourn to the psychological dystopia beyond. He was liable to hang, and so he fled, returning to Ireland, and to an anonymous, uncontroversial existence. On 4 January 1889, *Freeman's Journal* reported that Killeen had narrowly failed to secure a post as Medical Officer for the Clarecastle Dispensary District. In 1895, he failed to gain election to the position of Medical Officer for the Ennis Union Workhouse. One wonders whether professional disappointments of this sort paled in their significance, coming and going fairly easily amid the welcome triviality of Irish life as

Killeen studiously protected the guilty secret of his 1888 rampage. He lived on in Ennis until at least 1907, when his name finally disappears from the Medical Directory.

Of course, the deficiencies of Killeen's candidacy reflect those of many – if not all – of the other suspects. Thomas Bond, the doctor who reviewed all the case notes and performed the post-mortem on the wreckage of Kelly, discerned no necessary medical or anatomical expertise in the Ripper's mutilations, and the doctor-as-Ripper theory, in truth, lacks unanimous support at its root. There is no way of knowing the extent to which philosophical unquantifiables – Catholic sexual anxieties, for example – might have driven the killer; likewise, no evidence is available to speak of the specific circumstances which brought about the end of Jack the Ripper's spree, but the spontaneous remission of his desire to kill and mutilate seems unlikely. In psychology, there is such a thing as mirroring, but it does not imply the wholesale adoption of the mental processes of another individual.

★

The impregnability of the Ripper's enigma has made the parlour game of determining his identity into true crime's most popular and enduring pursuit. The academic and literary discipline surrounding the case – not always the rarefied version of the clubbable amateur hunt that it would like to pretend to be – has developed its own sine-wave energies, sometimes flush with confidence and rigour, sometimes anxious and readily susceptible to persuasion. Of all the events in Whitechapel's dark resumé, the murders of Jack the Ripper remain the most mysterious, and perhaps, to the student, the most rewarding; they offer a tapestry rich with preserved historical interest and the minutiae of private circumstances, but without the cosiness of a conclusion. It is hard to foresee an end to the great hunt-the-Ripper caucus race arriving soon, and at least one Ripper suspect of distinction, forced into the contest for dubious honours, might have been pleased to hear it.

Four

1898
(January)

In mid-century, Commercial Street scratched itself out through the slums of Whitechapel and Spitalfields, beginning opposite the junction of Red Lion Street and Whitechapel High Street, running north-by north-west to White's Row and Fashion Street, straightening towards north until Hanbury Street and Lamb Street, and then veering off north-by-north-west again to the junction with Shoreditch High Street and Norton Folgate. Its route had been designed to pass through some of the area's worst quarters – the rookeries around Rose Lane, for example – necessitating their demolition. The vague dream was of a better life, and of fewer rat-runs known only to the criminal underclass, but, in practice, displacing London's poorest people from one slum rarely had any better effect than to move them along to the next, increasing the already-prohibitive levels of overcrowding in the sections left alone by the planners' aspirations. By the time of Jack the Ripper, the dark roads running east and west off Commercial Street had acquired reputations they would never shake, as thousands of people drifted, purposeless and destitute, through the dismal common lodging houses of Thrawl Street, Flower and Dean Street, and Dorset Street.

The northernmost stretch of Commercial Street contained the higher numbers, and on the eastern side of this part of the road, just past the junction with Hanbury Street, there stood a row of four-storey buildings, peering down at the street below them. At number 118, which was part of this row, there was a coffee shop, Lockhart's; and it was just as she was passing this shop, at a little past five in the evening of Sunday 23 January 1898, that Annie Winderbank, a widow living in Cooney's Lodging House on Thrawl Street, heard something heavy land at her feet. She thought, perhaps, that some boys had thrown something at her, but the street was unusually quiet. Turning, she saw a baby girl, naked and bleeding, lying on the pavement to her right.

At the same time, with Mrs Winderbank walking past Lockhart's in the direction of Shoreditch, so Leah Limburg, aged nine, was walking towards her, and in the direction of Whitechapel. The day had been a dull one, and the sky was dark, but Leah suddenly perceived something plummeting towards her out of the gloaming. She tried to catch it, but missed, and not until it had hit the pavement did she see that it was a baby; now, it lay helplessly at her feet. Leah fled into the gathering blackness.

★

Annie Winderbank peered up at the windows of the buildings above her, striving for clear vision through the cataract she bore in one eye, but saw none open to the foggy winter dusk, and nobody looking back at her. The shops were shut, and there were few people around. A boy who passed by glanced down at the baby and remarked, 'Oh, it's a doll,' but Mrs Winderbank knew that it was not: she had heard the child crying. Mrs Winderbank looked up and down the street – not a policeman in sight. Leaving the baby where it was, she ran across the road to the Commercial Street police station.

In Mrs Winderbank's panicked absence, a crowd began to form around the baby as more passers-by discovered it for themselves. One of these was Elizabeth Spiller, a charwoman

Outside a lodging house
in Flower and Dean Street,
Spitalfields.

living at the White Hart on Great Pearl Street. As she reached the scene, she saw that the baby was bleeding from the head, and that blood was running from its mouth, and that it was trying to cry, but could not. It moved slightly, and Mrs Spiller picked the baby up, wrapped it in her apron, and set off for the police station.

In the meantime, Mrs Winderbank had managed to alert a policeman, and they were on their way back to the scene when they encountered Mrs Spiller. The baby was taken into the station, and the Divisional Surgeon, Franklin Hewitt Oliver, was called from his home on Kingsland Road. He arrived to find the baby breathing, well-developed, but gravely ill, and the child died minutes later. Oliver observed that the baby, in his own words, had 'received no skilled attention at birth'; to its body clung a residue of 'sebaceous material'; from its belly dangled four and a half inches of the umbilical cord, torn rather than cut at its loose end, and slick with blood. At the post-mortem, performed at the Whitechapel Mortuary on the morning of 25 January, Oliver determined that the baby's left thigh had broken in the middle. The brain had been badly injured, and part of it had emerged through an injury to the soft skull. It is perhaps a matter of grim chance that the other organs were undamaged – Oliver inflated the lungs, for example, and they floated in a bath of water.

★

On the evening of its death, the hunt began for the baby's mother. With Oliver, Inspector James Taylor of H Division went to the scene of its fall and they, too, looked up into the darkness at the rows of windows above them. It was, by now, after six in the evening.

At 116 Commercial Street, the excitement on the pavement outside had come to the attention of Abraham Clenowich and his wife Rachel. Abraham was a picture-frame maker, and his shop was situated on the ground floor of the building. At half past five, his daughter Alice, not yet ten years old, had come into the shop to tell him that 'a baby was on the stones'. Abraham left the shop and saw a small crowd outside Lockhart's, next door and to the north, before returning, unconcerned, to his work. Upstairs, in the kitchen, Rachel was told about the discovery of the baby by her thirteen-year-old daughter, Esther, some time after dusk. Rachel had gone down to the street, seeing a crowd of people there, but no baby.

By the time Dr Oliver and Inspector Taylor appeared at the street door, however, the circumstances surrounding the baby's sudden descent from dark skies must have become increasingly conspicuous, especially to Rachel. On the third floor of their house, a little before the arrival of the policeman and the doctor, she had found bloodstains, some near the lavatory, and some at the door to the back room. It was here, by night, that Rachel's three eldest children slept, together with her unmarried, twenty-two-year-old sister, Asneth Cohen, the four of them being distributed between two beds. Asneth had been alone in the room, and Rachel looked in through the door, which stood open. 'What is this?' she had asked, indicating the blood.

Asneth had blamed the mess on her period, but Oliver and Taylor, inspecting the third floor a while later, must have considered this an improbable excuse. The floor between the two beds appeared to have been washed, but Asneth's mattress was smeared with blood;

The site of 116 Commercial Street. (Author's collection)

concealed beneath the bed, a brick also bore blood stains. In the lavatory, the flooring was stained, and a trail of blood led from there to the front room, the room looking out into the darkness of Commercial Street, and to a sash window which was open two or three inches at the bottom. The bottom of the window was 2ft from the floor, and it was located towards the northern end of the west-facing wall – that is, close to the shared wall with Lockhart's, in front of which, 40ft below, the baby had been discovered. On the floor of the room, Oliver found a piece of cartridge paper marked with blood, and, below the window, two fire screens, on which the blood was still wet. A zinc pail stood to one side, with some old cloths in it.

But, amid the gore, Asneth herself was nowhere to be seen: between Rachel's visit to the third floor and the arrival of Oliver and Taylor, she had gone out, without her hat or her jacket, and neither Rachel nor Abraham had heard the front door shut as she had stepped, alone, into the gloom of the East End.

★

With Asneth missing, Rachel and her daughter Fanny – sixteen years of age, and one of the children who slept in the same room as Asneth – began to describe a pattern of strange behaviour which had evolved through the day, beginning when Fanny rose. Asneth had been in the habit of getting up at seven, but, that morning, she had complained to Fanny of feeling unwell, and Fanny left her in bed at nine o'clock. Asneth asked Fanny to bring her a pail of water with mustard in it – a familiar Victorian emetic – and Fanny did so at about ten. When she asked Asneth what was wrong, Asneth replied, apparently casually: 'Nothing much – I don't feel quite well.' Between ten and eleven, Rachel awoke and went down to the kitchen, and she was surprised not to find Asneth there. Fanny told Rachel that Asneth seemed unwell; Rachel recalled that Asneth had recently been complaining of chest pains, and sent Fanny back upstairs to deliver a cup of tea.

Fanny went upstairs twice more that afternoon – at one o'clock and three o'clock – finding Asneth asleep on both occasions. Rachel, too, went up to Asneth's room at a little after three, saying, 'What is the matter, my dear?' Asneth, though, was in bed, and reluctant to talk about her illness: 'I did not think it strange,' remarked Rachel, 'as it is always so with her.' Rachel stayed with Asneth, she remembered, for about four minutes, suspecting nothing at all. Later, she sent one of her daughters up to ask Asneth whether she would like anything to eat. Asneth, who had not ventured downstairs all day, declined the offer.

Then came the discovery of the baby in the street, Rachel's one-sided conversation with a muted Asneth, Asneth's unnoticed flight from the house, and the investigation of Oliver and Taylor, all of which left no remaining doubt as to the identity of the baby's mother, and its killer. It was all so sudden, but yet it defied easy interpretation. Abraham, clutching at the threads of logic, re-imagined an incident which had occurred before Christmas 1897, in which Asneth had annoyed him by 'moving a large quantity of pictures and papers in the front room where she had no business', but this was a poor way to nourish the theory – the only one to readily occur amid the grim scenery of the third floor – that Asneth had gone mad at or around the point of her child's delivery. Abraham himself admitted that he 'did not think it amounted to her being off her mind.' Rachel, for her part, reflected on Asneth's taciturn nature, but said that she had no relations who had been through the twilit systems of the Victorian asylums; Asneth carried no hereditary predisposition towards insanity, she thought, and the helplessness of Asneth's sister and brother-in-law to truly explain the events that had instantly overtaken them was unmistakeable. A matter of hours before, Rachel said, she had had 'no suspicion that she' – Asneth – 'was in the family way.'

★

Later on Sunday evening, Sarah Shadlofsky opened the door to her house at 35 Pedley Street, in the shadow of the railway running into Bishopsgate Goods Yard, and found Asneth Cohen huddled there. Mrs Shadlofsky had known Asneth for about four years, the same length of time that Asneth had lived with Rachel and Abraham; now, Asneth claimed to have quarrelled with them, and to have been thrown out of the house 'for nothing at all'. She asked Mrs Shadlofsky whether she could stay with her overnight. Mrs Shadlofsky had not seen Asneth for, she thought, six months, and noticed nothing unusual about her. She let her in.

Through Monday and into Tuesday morning, Asneth remained with Mrs Shadlofsky, punctuating her visit by sweeping the kitchen once, and otherwise, pathetically, rocking Sarah's little daughter Miriam. The overnight arrangement seemed to have become an indefinite one, and Mrs Shadlofsky hardly seems to have felt urgently inclined to let Rachel know where her sister was; but when Mrs Shadlofsky left the house at half past nine on the morning of 24 January, Asneth was sitting, dressed, on a chair, and, when she returned at ten, Asneth was gone, fearing, no doubt, that her whereabouts would, after all, be disclosed.

Two hours later, however, after shambling north through the dull morning, Asneth's willpower seemed spent; she arrived at 74 Dalston Lane, the home of Reuben and Sarah Clenowich, Abraham's cousin and his wife, and Sarah answered the door. Word of Asneth's predicament had reached her, but Sarah cautiously avoided piquing Asneth's suspicions.

'You look rather ill,' she said, matter-of-factly, to Asneth. 'What is the matter with you?'

'I had a misfortune,' admitted Asneth.

'What was it?' asked Sarah.

'Something came away from me which I threw out of the window,' said Asneth. 'It was a miscarriage.'

'What was it?' repeated Sarah.

'I don't know,' replied Asneth.

'I've heard a baby was thrown from a window,' tiptoed Sarah.

'Oh,' said Asneth, 'do they say it was a baby? I'm sure I don't know what it was.'

'Did you hear it cry?'

'No,' said Asneth. 'I felt quite dazed ... *mad* at the time.'

'Was anyone with you at the time?' asked Sarah.

'No.'

'Did your sister know anything about it?'

'No. I didn't tell her anything.'

'Did you tell your sister you were pregnant?'

'No,' replied Asneth. 'I didn't like to aggravate her.'

'What did you do with the stained clothes?'

'I hid them by some pictures,' said Asneth.

Sarah let Asneth into the house and related their too-real conversation to Reuben, and he went to fetch the police.

★

News of Asneth's apprehension reached Whitechapel just in time to inform the inquest into her daughter's death. Inspector Stephen White of Commercial Street police station and Dr Oliver were both in attendance at the hearing; Coroner Wynne Baxter opened proceedings, taking swift evidence of the discovery of the child on the pavement from Mrs Winderbank, and evidence of its passing away in the police station from Oliver, before adjourning the inquest until 14 February. White and Oliver immediately dashed north, finding Asneth in the police station on Dalston Lane, 'ill and apparently distressed'.

The doctor recommended that she be removed to an infirmary, and Asneth was taken in a four-wheeled cab to the Whitechapel Infirmary in Vallance Road, where she arrived at a quarter to four, to be cared for by Dr Herbert Larder. He examined Asneth, who struggled to understand his English, and whose own command of the language, at least in her unbalanced condition, went only as far as to say to him, 'I bleed'. Larder ascertained that Asneth had recently given birth, and treated her accordingly, thereafter keeping close watch on her, monitoring her state of mind. For the first two days, he thought, she was 'rather strange', and he instructed a special nurse to stay with her while her derangement lasted.

All that remains of Reuben and Sarah Clenowich's home at 74 Dalston Lane. (Author's collection)

By Friday 28 January, however, Asneth's agitation had given way to despair – she became intensely depressed, Larder noted, and especially at night, when she would be restless and cry frequently. As January became February, Asneth's condition remained parlous: one newspaper, published on the sixth, expressed 'grave doubts' that she would be well enough to appear at the resumed inquest hearing. When she did, on St Valentine's Day, battling against her enervated condition, she exhibited a 'frightened, dull appearance', seemed to be 'scarcely of average intellect', moaned when she was put into the dock, and gave no evidence on her own behalf. The coroner's jury returned a verdict of murder against her, with a rider recommending that her mental health be looked into – they had been troubled by her disturbed presentation at the hearing, but their remit did not extend to absolving her of responsibility for the death of her child.

This, perhaps, was all unhappy enough, and, according to Dr Larder's testimony to the jury, Asneth was, as yet, 'not quite recovered', but, on the morning of her appearance at the inquest, she had been met by Inspector White at the infirmary, and taken to the police station in Commercial Street. Here, White had told her that she would be charged with the murder of her daughter, and Asneth, at a low ebb, replied, 'Yes, I threw the baby out of the window. It was on Sunday night. I don't want them to kill me.' When the charge was read over by Inspector Taylor, she repeated her statement: 'I opened the window and threw the baby out.'

'She was not crying then,' snorted White, later, but this was scarcely in balance with the fact that he had omitted to caution her before she made her damaging, self-incriminating statements, and the scene as a whole seemed unsatisfying and unsympathetic: Inspector Taylor had seen Asneth sobbing, and mumbling something he could not make out; Oliver looked on, brow furrowed, and warned White that Asneth remained in a critical condition, but White had charged her anyway. A veteran of the Ripper crimes – a legend of limited veracity would suggest that he had 'seen' the killer strolling nonchalantly away from the scene of one of his murders – White's testimonials upon his retirement in 1900 told of a man who was talented, ingenious and determined; in Asneth's case, he may have had no choice but to charge her before the conclusion of the inquest, but her emotional vulnerability was achingly obvious, and the consequences of the charge inevitable. Asneth would be formally detained, and not in the Whitechapel Infirmary, from which she was theoretically entitled to walk free upon her theoretical recovery, but in the sickbay of Holloway Prison, with the possibilities of her discharge from the accusation or the granting of bail diminishing into nothing. Isolated, ill, and unpitied by the machinery of criminal justice, Asneth awaited her appearance before the magistrate.

The next day, Asneth was brought to the Worship Street Police Court, supported by a female searcher from the Commercial Street police station, to be the focus of a new round of painful enquiries; and, yet, it was from the darkness of her distress that hopeful flecks of light now began to emerge. Her supporters began to rise in her defence, or at least in mitigation, as the law loomed inflexibly over her. She was represented ably and energetically by Solomon Myers, a solicitor with offices on Wormwood Street, and a man for whom Asneth's case must have reawakened agonising memories of the murder of his own baby daughter, beaten and then poisoned to death by a fifteen-year-old housemaid, Emily Newber, in 1894. Myers expressed – and felt – sympathy for Asneth, although he had lost his own child to Newber's aimless cruelty. Behind him, in the public gallery, sat one Miss Levi, representing the Jewish Ladies' Society for Preventive and Rescue Work, a charitable body whose sensitivities had been piqued by newspaper reports of Asneth's desperate situation. At a second hearing, held on Saturday 27 February – an occasion characterised by the irascibility of Mr Cluer, the magistrate, who railed against the fees of the Yiddish interpreter, and the reluctance of Jewish witnesses to sign documents on the Sabbath – Asneth was committed to be tried at the Old Bailey, but, glancing up from the dock, she may already have perceived that she was not entirely friendless, and that some would fight to ensure that she should not be abandoned to the careless appetites of the legal system. Even while she was in Holloway, enduring the loneliness of the days before her trial, there were means of philanthropic support: Julius A. Goldstein, the Jewish minister attached to the prison, offered her wisdom and comfort; he liaised, on her behalf, with the prison's medical officer; he interpreted her Yiddish into English to ensure that her needs were met. He ensured that she was treated kindly in the infirmary, although he noted with regret that she remained in 'a dazed, deplorable condition', the deepest effects of her trauma failing to readily subside.

The trial, held at the Central Criminal Court on Thursday 10 March 1898, encapsulated the clash of cultures into which Asneth's child's short life and awful death had pitched its unhappy mother. In the dock was Asneth, a little over 5ft tall, dark skin and dark eyes, 'a profusion of jetty black hair', and better equipped to communicate in Yiddish than she was in English; on the bench, Mr Justice Grantham, sixty-two, and 'the picture of an English squire', to be seen riding 'booted and spurred, and with hunting crop in hand, on his iron-grey cob to the Royal Courts'. For Asneth, instructed by Solomon Myers, there appeared John Peter Grain and Leonard Kershaw – neither one a star name of the legal profession, Kershaw being regarded even by his obituarist in *The Times* as a 'poor speaker'; for the Crown, Charles Frederick Gill and Chartres Biron, lawyers of distinction and repute, who appeared in some of the most famous *causes célèbres* of their era – the trials of Oscar Wilde, the Royal Baccarat case, the Moat Farm Mystery, the ordeal of Adolf Beck.

Prior to the commencement of the proceedings, Myers and Asneth – supposing her condition to have allowed her to make any contribution at all – had decided that she would plead not guilty, rather than insane. This, at least, tested the quality of the prosecution's evidence, and in particular that of Franklin Oliver and Herbert Larder, who would be

The former Commercial Street Police Station, main entrance. (Author's collection)

The former Commercial Street police station. (Author's collection)

Pedley Street, the houses now gone. (Author's collection)

A corridor in Holloway prison, c. 1900.

required to speak as to Asneth's capacity to understand and appreciate the effects of her fatal actions. 'This was no doubt a first child,' said Oliver, cross-examined, his post-mortem on the baby's body apparently having carried him this far in his thinking; and he recognised Asneth's frailty upon her arrest in Dalston Lane. 'I came to the conclusion that she should not be then charged,' he went on. 'Her health was so much affected.'

Larder's examination of Asneth had been closer, and his monitoring of her fuller and more continuous. Upon her arrival at the infirmary, he said, Asneth required 'immediate attention'. Then he followed her progress, where he could. 'I examined her several times afterwards,' he explained. 'She was very weak, and is of a highly nervous temperament, and very likely under the circumstances might be subject to puerperal mania.'

For the jury, the crazed effects of puerperal mania – which modern medicine would describe as a post-natal or post-partum condition – neatly satisfied their desire to understand why a mother would throw her newborn baby out of a third-storey window: accordingly, they found Asneth guilty, but insane. This construction – peculiarly illogical and entirely legal – had been invented by Queen Victoria in 1882, as a means of expressing her annoyance that a madman who had shot at her had been found not guilty by reason of his flagrant insanity. English law had regularly attempted to separate the threads of intention and action, not always with much success, but, by the late Victorian period, it was becoming increasingly common for individuals who had spun off from reality, and who no longer knew whether what they did was right or wrong, to be acquitted of criminal offences where they were charged with them, and bound over for treatment instead. The suggestion that one could be found guilty *and* insane, both at the same time, was, as Viscount Dawson of Penn remarked during the second reading of the bill which became the 1938 Infanticide Act, 'fundamentally unsound,' and a step into a less-sympathetic past.

The Queen's indignation had muscled the verdict into law, despite the counsel of her nervous advisors.

But there was more. Asneth was 'temporarily irresponsible for her actions' – as *The Times* characterised the medical evidence – making her, conventionally, not guilty. But she had actually done what she was said to have done, and this point obviously troubled the jury. Further splitting of hairs was evidently possible in a case entangled in arcane legal possibilities, and the jurors clarified, if that be the word, that they believed her to be not guilty of murder, but guilty of throwing the child from the window – although, at the time, they thought, she was not responsible for her actions.

One can only imagine that the knotted, reflexive reasoning of the law, even if it made it relatively unscathed through the interpreter and into Yiddish, must have felt distant and indifferent to Asneth. Put simply, nobody considered her a murderer, and nobody felt that she had done anything deliberately wrong, or at least when in full control of her thoughts. But she was guilty anyway, and to be detained as a criminal lunatic. Again, though, there came a flurry of support; Mr Grain advised the judge that Miss Levi and the Jewish Ladies' Society were prepared to offer Asneth sanctuary, since, as a madwoman, and even a guilty one, she was not quite required to sit out a custodial sentence in a penitentiary. Mr Justice Grantham received the offer favourably, referring the decision to the Home Secretary. The *Jewish Chronicle* noted that Mrs Bramwell Booth had made a similar proposal on behalf of the Salvation Army, graciously turned down by the defence (who had plainly anticipated the verdict) in favour of Miss Levi's.

While the Home Secretary deliberated, however, Asneth was returned to Holloway, where she could be kept in the care of doctors and nurses as that hybrid of incompatible

Outside the Old Bailey at the turn of the century.

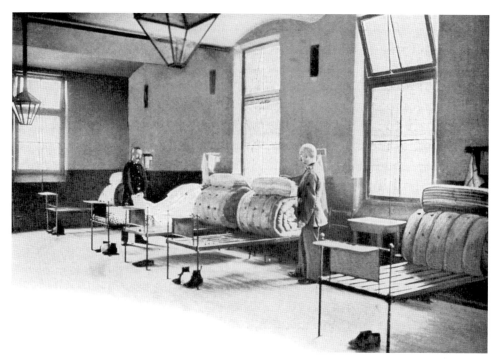

The infirmary at Holloway Prison, much as Asneth Cohen would have known it.

horrors, a criminal lunatic. Confused though it may have been, the Victorian justice system made honest attempts to provide treatment for those whose bruised mentality caused them to run to crime, and – in principle, at least – the mentally ill were not punished for offences which they had not committed voluntarily or with proper cognitive control. The list of criminal lunatics of the Victorian period is studded with part-famous names – Richard Dadd, a painter of vivid fairy scenes who killed his father; William Chester Minor, a paranoid surgeon who killed a man almost at random, and who later had the enforced leisure to contribute many examples of word-usage to the then-germinating *Oxford English Dictionary*; Christiana Edmunds, a mass poisoner, working mainly in the medium of chocolates laced with strychnine – and many of these individuals were linked by their time in Broadmoor Lunatic Asylum, Victorian England's premier repository for the dangerously insane. In its edition of Friday 25 March 1898, the *Jewish Chronicle* reported that the Home Secretary had come, finally, to a point of decision, and that Asneth had been removed to this forbidding institution.

★

She had been there since Tuesday 15 March, admitted bearing old scars to the legs, patches of her tongue stripped of their epithelium, and a few lice in her hair. An initial medical report described her as 'dull and stupid', although her initial distraction on transfer – 'she was very anxious and frightened' – had subsided within a month. Her family maintained contact with her through the perhaps unlikely offices of David Clenowich, Abraham's father, who generously expressed his willingness to care for Asneth, should she be released; this, however, was subject to Her Majesty's pleasure being made known. Asneth's stay was indefinite, and, though the months passed, still the monarch had not spoken.

A year into Asneth's institutionalisation, things looked more optimistic, although everything was relative. She had been physically healthy, although she was troubled by intermittent headaches; the debilitating effects of her emotional condition had 'gradually passed away', leaving her 'rational and tranquil' on inspection by the asylum's medical superintendent. In spite of her progress, this officer remained guarded about the prospects of Asneth's release: 'It is at present,' he wrote, 'too soon to say that she is fully and permanently recovered.' David Clenowich wrote again, via a proxy literate in English, offering to take her into his custody and, while he wrestled with the machinery of the Home Office, asking that important dates in the Jewish calendar be pointed out to Asneth, permitting her to observe certain festivities even in the timeless no-man's-land of Broadmoor. Rachel and another sister, Kitty Rosenberg, wrote in 1900, pledging their own support to David's campaign, and gradually, with Asneth's mental equilibrium holding firm, the doors to the outside began to be unlocked.

On 31 March 1900, Asneth was found to be 'not now insane', but 'facile, and easily influenced by others'. David Clenowich's credentials were examined: his capacity to provide the supervision Asneth required was balanced against a medical feeling that Asneth remained susceptible to a relapse into mania, but, with certain undertakings in place, her release was arranged. She left Broadmoor at eight o'clock in the morning on Thursday 31 May 1900, escorted by a plain-clothes attendant named Clarke. Together, they took a cab to Wellington College Station in Crowthorne, leaving Berkshire on the 08:27 morning

'Baby parade' in the exercise yard of a London prison: for Asneth, this tradition would have added a particular torment to her stay.

Grey Eagle Street as it appears today.
(Author's collection)

train for Cannon Street. From there, they took a second cab to 14 Grey Eagle Street, Spitalfields, the home of David Clenowich, and as he appended his usual mark to the certificate of receipt, Asneth returned to the society from which she had split in the momentary commission of her sad crime, twenty-eight months before.

Six months on, David wrote, as he was required to by the terms of Asneth's conditional discharge, to Broadmoor. 'I am pleased to say she enjoys very good health,' he enthused, 'and also behaves herself very well.' Similar reports were sent periodically, and the family, as they had promised in their letters, continued to care for the vulnerable Asneth – she seems, probably, to have spent time with Reuben and Sarah Clenowich, who remained in Dalston Lane, and where Asneth was recorded in the 1901 census, taken on the night of Sunday 31 March. She may have had a role in caring for Reuben and Sarah's children, Hetty, three, and Louis, two. Her rehabilitation proceeded without significant setbacks.

And then, on 8 May, Charles Thomson Ritchie, the Home Secretary, signed a Warrant of Absolute Discharge, freeing Asneth to emigrate. David had written to the asylum – though the letter is lost – requesting that she be given permission to remove to America, and Broadmoor had raised no objections. The SS *St Paul*, when it left Southampton on 6 June 1901, had on board a young woman clutching ticket number 2658, £2 in cash, and the address – 5 Orchard Street, New York – of the 'brother' (his identity abandoned to history) with whom, the ship's manifest said, she was to stay. The *St Paul* docked at Ellis Island on 15 June, and the past was, at last, behind Asneth, with thousands of miles of ocean between.

★

A few things to tidy up at the end of an unhappy case.

The baby had been born, probably, in the bedroom. The brick which had been left under the bed had been used to sever the umbilical cord – it broke the fibres of the cord, blood spilled out, and Asneth completed the operation either by hand, or by further jagged applications of the brick. She – bleeding – took the baby – bleeding – to the lavatory, but it quickly became clear that the blood they were losing was smearing itself widely, and the only way to minimise its spread was to get the baby out of the house. This Asneth did by opening the window, and 'throwing' it, to use her own description, and not 'dropping' it, from the third floor. The baby landed in front of Lockhart's shop, a few feet along the street

The SS *St Paul*. (Author's collection)

towards Shoreditch, suggesting that Asneth had given it a little northward impetus. Asneth had managed to conceal her pregnancy, even from those sleeping in the same room as her, by virtue, one newspaper said, of her naturally stout physique.

And lastly to the question of the baby's father. At the inquest, Abraham Clenowich had recalled that Asneth had lately kept the company of a 'paperhanger and decorator', whom he discreetly refrained from identifying by name. He knew it, however – Asneth had told him when he visited her at the Whitechapel Infirmary on Tuesday 8 February. 'She did not say whether she had been keeping company with him up to the present time,' he concluded; and there the coroner's curiosity seems to have desisted, leaving the father of the baby anonymous to posterity.

Or read it another way. Asneth told nobody of her pregnancy, but she seems to have been particularly afraid of 'aggravating' her sister Rachel. Her refuges, following her flight from Commercial Street, were both, apparently, Abraham's connections: Sarah and Reuben Clenowich by, as it were, blood, and Sarah Shadlofksy because her husband, Henry, was a glazier who had had, no doubt, some professional interaction with Abraham, a picture-frame maker. If there was any sympathy to be had, not least after Asneth's incarceration, it was mainly from Abraham, or from those who knew him. Even the mysterious brother to whose American residence she was eventually destined was more likely a Clenowich – or, an outside bet, a Shadlofsky – than a Cohen. And then return to Abraham's coy inquest testimony: 'She kept company with a paperhanger and decorator. I don't know whether the affair has been going on up to the present time... She told me the name of the father of the child. She did not say whether she had been keeping company with him up to the present time.' Rachel never claimed to know – or to have been told – the identity of the baby's enigmatic father.

Perhaps there never was a decorator; perhaps Abraham had special cause to protect the secret of the paternity of Asneth Cohen's daughter.

Five

1898
(November)

Ten years had passed since the Ripper's reign of fear, but, in Millers Court, legend had it that the walls of Mary Jane Kelly's room were long smeared with her blood, an awful – perhaps indelible – memorial to her murder. Sleeping in the room above the wreckage that morning had been one Elizabeth Prater: according to her testimony at the inquest into Kelly's segmentation, she was awakened at four by her kitten walking across her neck, and she heard a faint cry of 'murder', to which she paid no attention. In the early 1890s, Prater was to be found still living in Millers Court, in one of the rooms opposite, and she led an impromptu tour to Kelly's room when a journalist arrived to investigate social conditions in London's East End. She had already told the press that she would never forget the sight of Kelly lying murdered on the bed, which she had glimpsed through a window while ostensibly on a trip out for water. The police were then inside the room, gazing helplessly at the dismal ruin before them. But Prater had been reaching a crescendo of nervous anxiety even before Mary Jane Kelly's death: returning to her room at half past one in the morning on 9 November 1888, she had barricaded herself in with two tables jammed firmly against the door.

So, with Elizabeth Prater boxed securely in upstairs, Mary Jane Kelly had opened her door to death, and, when the local terror eventually dwindled, black humour and morbid curiosity replaced it. One wonders how helpful Prater found the attitude of later residents of Millers Court, who, the aforementioned journalist wrote, 'grew voluble' on the subject of the killing, 'and seemed to gloat over the hideous details, like birds of prey.' It was 'horrible beyond expression'. There was 'a sort of apathetic, matter of fact wickedness' in their retellings, and, if the description of the scene is an accurate one, Prater's close call scarcely seems to have attracted the empathy of her peers. Who cared for the survivor's story? And, it was true, she had left it, pursuant to an attempt to reunite with her husband, but the room at the top of the stairs, the room above Kelly's, had been the safest place in

The service road which now stands on the site of Dorset Street. (Author's collection)

Elizabeth Prater's world on the most dangerous night of her life. Within ten years, however, it too would be the venue for murder.

★

By 1898, Kate Marshall's story already told of the inability of the Victorian prison system to rehabilitate the damaged individuals who passed through its dank corridors. Her first sentence, handed down in 1879, when she was twenty-five, had been for cutting another woman's face with a broken plate; at or around the same time – and rather tellingly – she had also stabbed her own father, injuring him. More imprisonments followed on the heels of her release: two, set apart by little more than a year in the mid-1880s, were for attacking two members of the same family, and, strange to tell, a third member of the family, David Roberts, still went on to marry Kate's younger sister Eliza. Kate had her own dysfunctional, unsettled relationship with a man called Christopher Hayes, who went by the unusual nickname of 'The Flower of the Flock', and who worked as a porter at Spitalfields Market. In 1883, a policeman had intervened in an argument between Kate and Hayes, and Kate had assaulted him, earning herself another period in prison. In 1889, she was given eighteen months with hard labour – her longest sentence

A scene from Millers Court. (*The Illustrated London News*, 10 January 1891)

to date – for wounding a woman with a knife; in 1894, another three months, under the same conditions, for another assault on the police. In May 1895, she caved Hayes's head in when he refused to get her more beer in the Britannia, at the corner of Dorset Street, and it was probably after this incident that he had to wear a silver plate in his skull, so bad was the damage. When she was arrested by PC Masterton for this offence, she apparently told him that she had meant to kill. Given five years with hard labour, she was out of prison again by about September 1898 on a ticket-of-leave, and, at a loose end, moved in with her sister Eliza and her brother-in-law David.

Eliza and David had had eight children, but, by 1898, only three were still alive; their two girls were being cared for by Dr Barnardo. In the spring of that year, with their remaining son, they had moved into 19 Millers Court, formerly Elizabeth Prater's room, but now renumbered, on the first floor and at the back of 26 Dorset Street. The arrival of Kate after her incarceration added to the claustrophobic atmosphere – the room was probably no more than 12ft by 10ft, footprinted on Mary Jane Kelly's former home below, and the Roberts family were now relegated to a mattress on the floor, as Kate took the bed. The pressure soon began to tell, and Eliza and Kate 'were not, as a rule, on the best of terms', as David Roberts later reflected.

But nor, by now, were David and Eliza. One Friday night in October or early November, in a drunken rage, he set about her with a poker. She went to the hospital with her head split open, and he was charged at the Worship Street Police Court, and bound over to keep the peace when Eliza declined to have him prosecuted. Tensions continued to rise, and while David's trade – painting and decorating – took him out of the house, giving him a pressure valve, Eliza and Kate often remained indoors making whips, forced into each other's company. When they did go out, it was to sell the whips they had made, and this soon became a competitive process, with each woman denigrating the commercial performance, and the quality of the workmanship, of the other. They would 'quarrel and jangle ... about their work,' David remembered, heightening the sense of stress in their confined quarters. On the day of David and Eliza's tenth wedding anniversary, Saturday 26 November 1888, he left the room at half past seven in the morning, and returned at half past six in the evening, 'not sober and not drunk', in his own words. Eliza and their son were there – Eliza went out to sell her whips at 7:30 p.m., leaving David and the boy alone in the room. At 10:15 p.m., with neither woman back from the streets, they went to bed.

★

Eliza and Kate were in the Britannia by eleven, or shortly thereafter. Annie Blanche Haysman was behind the bar, and remembered them taking a glass of mild ale each. They did not seem drunk, Annie thought, or on bad terms – indeed, she found them 'very friendly', and the sisters left contentedly at 11:45 p.m., apparently detouring past the entrance to Millers Court in order to get a quart can of ale from the Blue Coat Boy, a little further down Dorset Street. They eventually arrived back at 19 Millers Court at midnight, finding David and the boy lying in the bed – taking the opportunity to escape the mattress on the floor – and with the gas light on. David noticed that the women were 'the worse for drink': this augured badly, although he accepted a glass of beer which Eliza poured for him from the can.

With the women now fuelled by alcohol, the inevitable argument about the proceeds of their whip sales began. Kate, whom David considered the more profitable salesperson, but who was only an occasional rent-payer – fourpence here, sixpence there – told Eliza, provocatively, 'I got you four shillings for your work and what more do you want?' Eliza responded with barbs about the rent and, after five or six minutes of mutual goading, a fight broke out. Kate seized Eliza by the hair, and they fell to the floor, overturning the table, from which the crockery fell and broke. David, pushed as far as he wished to be by the grim predictability of the drunken, midnight row, got up out of bed wearing only a shirt and no trousers, to separate them. This done, he returned to bed and comforted the child, who was upset by the scene; and peace descended.

But the ceasefire was only temporary. Kate, a volatile character with a history of uncontrollable surges of temper, took a broken jug from the heap of junked crockery on the floor and began smashing out the small, square panes in the sash window which looked into Millers Court. Four panes had gone (in addition to the two already cracked) when Kate turned to Eliza, saying either, 'Is that what you mean?' or, perhaps, 'You thing, I will give you something for this,' and we can suppose that, if it was the latter, then 'thing' was not the word used. She rushed at her younger sister, hitting her in the chest with her right hand. There was a beat of silence, and then Eliza said, 'Dave – she has stabbed me.'

KATE MARSHALL.

(Courtesy of Robert Clack.)

Now David sprang out of bed, grabbing a struggling, inflamed Kate by the wrists, as Eliza's bodice crimsoned from the wound to her chest. Gradually, David and Kate fought their way out onto the 9ft landing outside the door to their room; here, adjacent to the stairs, there was a windowless storage room sometimes used as shelter by the destitute, and, directly opposite the door to number 19, the wooden partition which sectioned off room 20. David kicked at the partition to summon help from the occupants, and Charles Amery emerged. He had heard the raised voices; he opened his door to see David and Kate lying on the floor, David holding her wrists apart as she tore frantically at the hem of his shirt. Plainly, Kate was in a state of histrionic frenzy, but David managed to relieve her of an old shoemaker's knife, which she clasped in her right hand, and passed it up to Amery, saying, 'Take this.' Amery did, and found it wet and sticky with blood. Moments later, he saw Eliza stagger out of room 19 and collapse at the top of the stairs.

Mary Johnson – Amery's common-law wife, seeing all this from their room – ran down the stairs and out of the door into the passageway, through Dorset Street, and across Commercial Street to Christ Church, where she found PC Alfred Fry on fixed point duty. Fry hurried to the crazed scene, finding Eliza unconscious at the top of the stairs, and Kate and David still grappling on the landing. He blew his whistle to attract assistance, and PC William Bartropp arrived from Dorset Street in moments; word of the tumult reached Brushfield Street, too, parallel with Dorset Street and a block to the north, and PC James Randall ran from there. Fry had, by this time, taken the still-struggling Kate from David, and he held her with 'great difficulty'; David, who had been left naked by Kate's feverish attentions to his shirt, which she had eventually torn off him, had repaired to his room to put on some clothes. Bartropp was sent to fetch a doctor; Randall took the knife from Amery, and managed to get Kate down the staircase, and up the road to the police station on Commercial Street through a curious crowd of onlookers.

This left only Eliza, who was motionless at the top of the stairs, pale, her lips blanched, her bodice saturated with dark blood. She was attended by Dr David Hume, who had been brought from his house on White Lion Street, and Hume had her removed to Amery's room. Eliza was laid on the floor and given some brandy and water as a stimulant, which she managed to take; but the doctor found that 'there was no appreciable effect', and, in David's presence, Eliza died, approximately ten minutes after she had been wounded.

The next evening, David was interviewed by the *Daily News* – the rapidly-developing sensation of the story superseding the insensitivity of approaching the bereaved husband – and his three-year-old son apparently cried throughout, 'Where's Mummy? Is Mummy coming?'

★

The next day, at the Whitechapel Mortuary, David Hume and Frank Hewitt Oliver, the Divisional Surgeon, performed the post-mortem on the body of Eliza Roberts. She was thirty-six years old, well-nourished, with a somewhat stern demeanour, but bearing none of the marks of anger which scrawled themselves across Kate's jagged face. There was a stab wound to the right side of her chest, an inch below the sternum, which penetrated through the muscle situated between the first and second ribs. This was the fatal blow, angled downwards and inwards: at its deepest point, it had punctured Eliza's right lung, causing it to collapse; the damage to the blood vessels caused a haemorrhage; shock set in; Eliza bled away. Beer was found in the stomach; several defence wounds scarred the arms and legs, probably inflicted in the opening shots of the fight, before the women were separated by David. The inquest, held on Tuesday 29 November at the Whitechapel Coroner's Court, found a verdict of murder against Kate Marshall *in absentia* – she had been contacted via the authorities at Holloway Prison, to which she had been removed on a police charge of murder, but had waived her right to attend.

MRS. ROBERTS.

(Courtesy of Robert Clack.)

At the committal hearings held at the Worship Street Police Court, however, a competing story began to emerge. Kate was now in statutory attendance, looking (at least initially) weak and miserable, according to the *Penny Illustrated Paper*, and dressed in a 'shabby black dress' and veil which pastiched mourning for her deceased sister. She had acquired a solicitor, a Mr George Eric Havelock of 9 Trinity Street in Borough, to whom she had told a very different version of events. At the third hearing, a vehement *tour de force*, Kate held court against the burden of accusation. In her rendition, David Roberts was a drunken bully, and the incident with the poker was only the most public of a series of more private abuses. At one o'clock on the afternoon of the murder, she said, Roberts had returned home spoiling for a fight, and offering to split open the other side of Eliza's head. He had conceived of the idea that Eliza and Kate were supplementing their whip sales with prostitution, telling them, 'If there is such a person as the fucking almighty God, he'd take you pair of whores out of my sight.' He left, returning at seven, drunk and angry. This time, he lunged at Eliza with the iron hearth fender, but Kate stood in the way to defend her.

According to Kate, Roberts then produced a pawn ticket for a glass cutter's diamond, which he wanted Eliza to sell. Kate – improbably characterising herself as the voice of law-fearing reason – advised her sister to have nothing to do with it, speculating that the diamond had been stolen. The women hurried out to sell their whips, leaving Roberts – intoxicated, penniless and thwarted – in the room. They stayed out until a quarter to midnight, hoping that he would sober up in the meanwhile. On their return, however, they found Roberts in bed, drinking from a can of beer. Immediately the abuse began again: Roberts accused his wife and sister-in-law of selling themselves for sex; 'Drunken bastard,' Eliza retorted. By now Roberts had reached the peak of his fury, but, inconveniently for her case, Kate did not quite see whatever happened next. 'It was done so quick,' she said.

Still, the rest of the story fell into place very naturally. Rather than seeing Roberts struggling with a murderous Kate, Amery had in fact witnessed Kate struggling to rein

Outside a London coroner's court at the time of the crime.

in a murderous Roberts. She clung to his leg to prevent him from approaching poor Eliza again – Eliza herself had got as far as the landing, exclaiming, 'Oh, Jesus,' and rapidly draining of colour. When the policemen arrived, Roberts, still entwined with Kate, said, 'I charge her, she's stabbed my wife,' and Kate, suddenly accused of a crime she did not commit, was too startled to really deny it. 'It sent me silly,' she said, and both sides agreed that she moaned something approximating, 'Liz, Liz. What have I done to you? Why don't you speak to me?' In Roberts's version of events, this was the instant, useless remorse of the arrested killer, doomed to hang; in Kate's version, the emphasis fell elsewhere in the sentence – 'What have *I* done to you?' Intonation was everything. 'Of course, I meant that I had done nothing,' insisted Kate.

This was powerful, evocative stuff, but essential parts of it failed to tally with the other evidence. Kate had no reasonable explanation for the movement of the knife between its various custodians, for instance. She did not see it in David's hand during the struggle, she said; she later saw it passed to PC Randall by either Amery or David, but she could not say which. Charles Amery, however, had told the inquest that he had seen David snatch the knife out of Kate's hand, and received it from him while Kate continued to struggle, and that he, Amery, had passed the knife on to Randall upon Kate's arrest. Amery stuck to this concise, uncomplicated version of events throughout. He also testified to having heard 'a crash of glass' at about the time Kate was alleged to have put out the windows; corroborating this was the evidence of Frank Oliver, who had attended the scene on the night of the crime and noticed that the windows were all smashed. But Kate's recollection was different: 'I don't remember any windows being broken. There were none to break. They were all paper.' Neither the glass cutter's diamond nor the pawn ticket purportedly relating to it was ever found: 'I have never been able to have a glass cutter's diamond,' said David. And from where did Kate think that David had got his weapon? 'By sitting up in bed,' she explained, 'Roberts could easily reach the knife... It was usually kept on a little shelf at the foot of the bed near the window.' David rejected the idea: 'It was kept as a rule in the prisoner's pocket ... I never had it in my hand before.' Kate had bought the knife two days before, saying that it would do for work.

The case went forward to the Old Bailey, where, on Thursday 13 January 1899, after a two-day trial, Kate Marshall was found guilty of murder, and sentenced to death. She stuck with the defence she had presented at Worship Street, despite its weaknesses, and made a great scene in court. The 1898 Criminal Evidence Act had granted those on capital charges the right to speak in their own defence; this caused consternation in some quarters of the legal profession, who saw in the public an unschooled propensity to accidental self-incrimination. Kate blossomed

SCENE OF THE MURDER.

(Courtesy of Robert Clack.)

in the spotlight, again fashioning her romantic, heroic character in a narrative dominated by the dark, malicious, but ultimately exaggerated, figure of Roberts. The jury took only thirty minutes to return with their verdict, and, with the judge, Mr Justice Darling, looking grimly out at her from beneath the black cap, Kate flew into panicked histrionics. Asked if she had anything to say, she juxtaposed her dismal record of infractions against the person – elucidated in court under the provision of the same 1898 Act – with the twenty-seven stab wounds she bore on her own body, the scars of a stormy life. Violence was endemic in her existence, but, she said, her past convictions had been acquired in desperate acts of self-defence. 'I say before the Lord Jesus, the Trinity, and Heaven, that I am innocent of this dreadful charge,' she protested. 'God knows, and I call upon Him, my defender, that I am innocent before the whole world of this crime. Do with me what you will; I am innocent.' On being led from the dock to await execution, her objections grew shriller: 'Oh! Jesus; this is perfect murder. Oh my God! Oh Liz! Oh Dave Roberts, you killed my sister! Where is God? I call upon Him!' Up in the courtroom, her exhortations could be heard for some time after she had been removed to the cells.

★

In *Lloyd's Weekly Newspaper*, on Sunday 22 January 1899, it was reported that Kate Marshall was 'in a depressed state of mind and low condition generally. Her terrible position has had a marked effect on her.' She languished in the condemned cell in Newgate Prison, relying on peripatetic visits from the Roman Catholic priest of Holloway and what was called the 'hospital diet' for spiritual and physical sustenance. In the free world, Samuel Barnett, the reformer and clergyman, wrote to *The Times* from Commercial Street's Toynbee Hall, emphasising the link between social indifference, poverty and crime, of which he considered Kate's case an example. Less salubriously, Kate's solicitor, Havelock, was in Bow Street seeking the knife with which Eliza Roberts had been killed; the magistrate decided that Havelock wanted it as a morbid relic of an unedifying case, and refused to give it over.

London jurors waiting to view a body as part of an inquest.

The days ticked past, and execution loomed.

Eventually, however, a reprieve arrived. The jury, in their verdict, had recommended mercy on the basis that the crime had been committed drunkenly and spontaneously: Havelock, between souvenir-hunting excursions, found the time to submit a petition on Kate's behalf, arguing that the jury's finding had been tantamount to a conviction for manslaughter, an offence which did not carry a capital penalty. The hazy interpretation of the Criminal Evidence Act, still to be bedded down in common law, perhaps made the weight of these arguments, however: mentioning Kate's previous convictions was liable to be prejudicial, unless the defence were running an argument which imputed some malfeasance to the prosecution witnesses, and while the precise meaning of the Act was determined through juridical practice, reprieves were handed down where necessary. In Kate's case, although she had accused David Roberts of the murder, it was not clear that this constituted an 'imputation' under the new law. The reprieve was signed on 26 January, five days before the scheduled execution, and Kate's sentence was reduced to penal servitude for life. In 1901 and 1911, she was recorded in prison in Aylesbury, Buckinghamshire, and on both occasions she described herself as a whipmaker in normal life, although her career was fairly obviously on long-term hiatus.

★

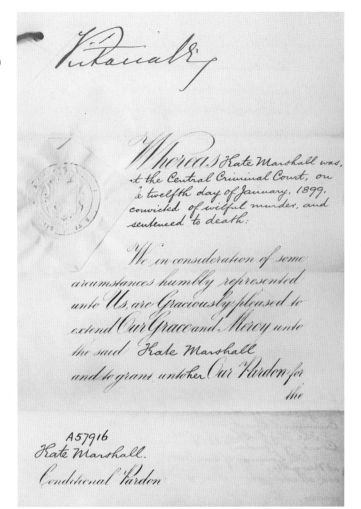

Right Kate Marshall's reprieve, signed by Queen Victoria. (The National Archives, ref. CRIM 1/582/15)

Below Aylesbury Prison, Kate Marshall's destination following her reprieve. (Author's collection)

There is no doubt about the propriety of the verdict, but the direction of Kate's defence deserves further reflection. There had been some kind of relationship between the Roberts family and the Marshall family for a solid fifteen years before the murder. In court, David Roberts observed that, although he and Eliza had married in 1888, their eldest child was fifteen, and apparently still living under the charitable auspices of Dr Barnardo. If this is right, Eliza and David had indeed been cohabiting for 'fifteen or sixteen years', as he said, although they had been married for only ten of them. Kate had been on the scene at the outset: in May 1883, she had been given a two-month sentence, with hard labour, for attacking David Roberts's sister; in October 1884, she was sentenced to ten months for wounding his brother with a knife, and claimed, in retrospect, that she had intended the blow to be for David himself. Even in the few months in which they lived together at 19 Millers Court, David claimed that Kate had 'very often threatened to stab me'.

But yet, despite the risk she posed, Kate was serially welcomed back into the fold. The room above Mary Jane Kelly's was hardly palatial (it served, one newspaper wrote, 'for bedroom and parlour and kitchen and hall'), but David 'did not interfere' when Kate moved in and added to the overcrowding. One report has it that Eliza 'called a doctor, and, out of her scanty means, helped her sister regain her health,' for Kate had come out of prison the worse for her experience. David, on the other hand, noted the frequent 'jangling' between the sisters, and claimed that they were on generally bad terms.

Viewed one way, the murder of Eliza Roberts seemed the summation not only of the proximal effects of the congestion in the tiny room, but of a dammed-up surge-tide of feeling going back a decade and a half. She was prone to sexual jealousy, but, perhaps, of a rather scattergun kind. Her 1889 conviction had been for an assault on a woman she had found in the company of Christopher Hayes. By comparison, years later at her capital trial, her barrister, Dr Edward Counsel, asked David Roberts whether he was not engaging in extra-marital relations with one Annie Jackson, who shared room 20 with Amery and Mary Johnson. Roberts denied it, but it is natural to suggest that this particular 'imputation' originated with Kate. Why should she have wanted to stab him in 1884, when his brother got in the way? Why did he not put his foot down when his unbalanced and violent sister-in-law came to stay in his cramped and crabbed little room in Millers Court? Seen in this context, their struggle on the landing – he naked but for the shirt she then tore from his body – assumes symbolic proportions. In the most desperate corners of the East End, modesty was a redundant affectation, disappearing arithmetically with privacy. Roberts had already lifted himself out of bed once, lacking clothing below the waist, to stop Kate and Eliza arguing before the *contretemps* spilled over into murder. Social conditions in the Victorian slums ensured that a graphic, physical intimacy which could not have been tolerated in some wealthier sections of society was achieved accidentally, or incidentally, as well as deliberately, by people for whom the moral schemata of the times had long given way to the instincts of survival. We ought not to confuse Kate and David's poverty with anything more salacious, but the whispered undertones of the crime for which they are remembered may just suggest that, with her final confinement to prison in 1899, there ended a complex and finally destructive relationship, part love, part hate, and a grim fable of unforgiving times.

Six

1909

In the popular imagination, Whitechapel groped through the late Victorian and Edwardian periods enveloped in an opaque fog, with occasional blurs of light – dim gas lamps, or the cut-glass windows of public houses – shimmering here and there in the darkness. The ambient effects of the local manufacturing industries which dominated the area doubtless contributed to whatever truth the idea ever possessed, but this enduring *leitmotiv* of impenetrable gloom, perpetuated through the cinema and literary pot-boilers, is probably best understood as a convenient analogue for the strange, shadowy lives of the East End's inhabitants. The nooks of Whitechapel were the anonymous hinterland of the world's wealthiest city, an alchemist's crucible in which identities melted, and in which new identities formed. Yards away, in the Square Mile, a separate class of people established and fought for their reputations, clinging to the concrete and the unchanging as the props of their prosperity; across the border and into old Middlesex, countless folk emerged as if from nowhere, and dissolved promptly into the great, mysterious throng. Their existences were shrouded – metaphorically – in the fog which supposedly choked the streets. Kitty Roman was one of these human *tabulae rasae*, starting again in the facelessness of East London; history conspired with her in her quest for oblivion, misremembering her surname, and rendering it Ronan.

This was despite the fact that, in 1912, not quite three years after her death, an attempt had been made to carve the name of Kitty Roman in stone. A play of, seemingly, rather didactic and religious sensibilities had been written by Edith Lyttelton, and in this play, called *Peter's Chance*, a character by the name of Kitty Roman appeared. On stage, Kitty was a thief who spoke in a coarse, stylised manner, all missing aspirants and frantic urgency; other players described her variously as a 'lyin' hussy' or, more flatteringly, a 'fine, strapping sort of girl'. *The Times* found Florence Lloyd's portrayal of the part of Kitty 'vivid and attractive', but Huntly Carter, writing for the *New Age*, thought that the moralising tone of the drama marred its effect. The play was set in a mission house in Stepney, but, Carter grumbled, it was obvious that Mrs Lyttelton, the dramatist, had 'never seen the inside of an East-End mission house' except in her 'Park Lane imagination'. The two-dimensional presentation of Kitty was particularly unsympathetic – as the play draws to a close, she stabs a confederate whose sudden pangs of religious principle have prevented him from stealing the plate from the chapel to which the mission is attached, and he dies on the chapel steps in a rather symbolic manner. 'I never saw a sillier play,' said Carter and, as far as one can judge, *Peter's Chance* is rarely, if ever, performed any longer. But the immortalisation of Kitty Roman as a murderer in a sanctimonious Edwardian drama did provide, at least, an interesting inversion of history; for the truth of it was that, in 1909, in Spitalfields, Kitty herself had been found cruelly murdered.

★

In simpler times, Kitty had been Katie, and she and her father Andrew had arrived in London from New York in the late 1880s or early 1890s. Both were Americans by birth; the third part of the trinity, Katie's mother, had apparently died when Katie herself was still in her formative years. Andrew, then, had hoped for a new start, settling in Fulham, in West London, and quite quickly developing a relationship with one Annie Monk, who became Katie's *de facto* stepmother. Katie went to school on Lillie Road, but academia probably did little to calm a temperament described, albeit in retrospect, as 'restless and wayward'. Neither Andrew nor Annie had any enthusiasm for the idea, but Katie apparently insisted on going into domestic service. In 1902 or 1903, she left home with this end in mind, but, by about 1907, she had drifted eastwards, through the more salubrious suburbs, to Spitalfields. By the spring of 1908, she was living in, or in the menacing vicinity of, Duval Street (formerly Dorset Street), and, on Monday 24 May 1909, she agreed to take the rent – five shillings weekly – on 12 Millers Court. This first-floor room, measuring a parsimonious 12ft by 12ft and 2ins, looked out through one of its two windows onto the room in which Eliza Roberts had been stabbed to death and, below that, Mary Jane Kelly's charnel house. The furniture in Kitty's room – what furniture there was – had seen better days, and her austere living conditions contrasted with the pride she apparently took in her personal appearance. Contemporaries reflected approvingly on her cleanliness, and she was known as a demure, quiet figure, not addicted to alcohol, who made her living by ironing sheets in common lodging houses or by selling flowers outside Aldgate Station.

Still, though, this was hardly the life for which Kitty had originally hoped. As her fortunes worsened, so she wrote to her father and stepmother less and less often, and she visited them only rarely; when she did, she concealed the truth of her circumstances, saying nothing more than that she was 'happy and comfortable' in service. In fact, the recourse to prostitution had become sadly inevitable as Kitty struggled to make ends meet, and, two days after taking up the financial burden of 12 Millers Court, Kitty took home one Henry Benstead, who had been, until that moment, the boyfriend of a friend of Kitty's named Lily Cook. Benstead underwent a rapid shift of allegiances, and lived with Kitty from this point on. This arrangement helped with the rent, although Benstead was not what one might have called lucrative. He sometimes found casual work as a newspaper vendor, or as a market porter, but he was probably more accustomed to living a hand-to-mouth existence funded by the earnings of the prostitutes with whom he cohabited. Benstead affected a relaxed attitude to the matter, saying that he thought that Kitty 'occasionally went out soliciting prostitution, but I have never seen her, and it was not with my consent.'

At one o'clock on the afternoon of 1 July 1909, Benstead left Kitty in their room and went to his father's home in Bethnal Green: money was again at a premium, and he was hoping for a spot of paternal charity. Mr Benstead senior, however, was not at home, and it took until four o'clock for the younger man to locate his father in the Crown and Anchor in Buxton Street. Given that the drink was already flowing, Benstead *fils* was perhaps lucky to extract two shillings from Benstead *père*, and, equipped with this sum, he left the pub, and went, in his own words, for 'a walk round'. It was an aimless Thursday, and Benstead had little on his mind, and little mind to look for work. At seven, he pitched up at the Bee Hive Lodging House on Brick Lane, a vast dormitory set on the corner with Princelet Street, seeking the company of its residents rather than the dubious luxury of its beds. Shortly after nine, he went out again into the gathering darkness of Spitalfields, and passed down Fournier Street in the direction of Commercial Street.

Turning the corner, with the Ten Bells to his right and Christ Church to his left, Benstead spotted Kitty walking south along Commercial Street; with her was a friend, known to Benstead as Suey Smith. He followed the women, 'trying to hear what they were talking about', and caught up with them at the junction of Flower and Dean Street. Kitty told Benstead that she was taking Suey to the chemist on Wentworth Street – Suey, apparently, 'wanted some ointment'. Benstead, seemingly uninterested in Suey's rather

Brick Lane, a noisy, busy thoroughfare cutting through the East End.

The Ten Bells, whose name is always associated with the Ripper case, although its links to the affair are relatively slight. (Author's collection)

venereal-sounding complaint, asked Kitty if she had had anything to eat. She had not, and Benstead gave her a shilling – or perhaps a few pennies more – telling her to buy herself some supper. 'Yes,' said Kitty, 'but what about the rent?'

If the women now went off to Wentworth Street so, too, did Benstead. He loitered here until, between eleven o'clock and half past, he returned to the Bee Hive, where he had a cup of tea with a man named Barnet Sheinisohn, and chatted about nothing in particular with a couple of other men. As it rolled round to half past one in the morning, the night porter, Tom Stanton, politely asked whether the clutch of men in his kitchen had had any thoughts about going to bed – they took the hint, and Stanton saw Benstead leave the Bee Hive via the side door into Princelet Street. With one of his companions from the Bee Hive – 'a Jewish boy' – in tow, Benstead headed towards Millers Court.

Kitty, in the meantime, had shaken off Suey and returned to be within steps of her cramped bedroom, obviously on the lookout for prospective clients. At half past ten, she was spotted, alone, by PC Herbert Bursted outside the Britannia, on the corner of Duval Street and Commercial Street. Bursted had been on the Spitalfields beat long enough to have figured out some of Kitty's habits. He had seen her accompanying men to her lodgings, and he knew that it was her practice 'to stand outside the Britannia nightly up till about closing time.' She would also walk occasionally to the other side of the road, and it was here, sitting on the stone outside the church, that she was spotted shortly before midnight by Rose Buckwell, an acquaintance who lived in Quaker Street. The two girls – Rose was twenty, but already, in her own words, 'an unfortunate' – spoke briefly, and then Rose went on her way, saying, 'Good night, God bless you.' At the corner of Fournier Street, however, she turned around, and saw Kitty being harassed by 'a couple of what I believe to be Yiddish lads.' They had their arms around Kitty's waist and neck, but Kitty wriggled free of them, and joined Rose at the corner of the street. The men, whoever they were, passed on towards Shoreditch, and the women separated, with Kitty standing alone in the gloomy midnight shadows of Christ Church.

An hour and a half later, on the same corner, Benstead parted from his companion and crossed into Duval Street. He walked through the archway into Millers Court, and found the ground-floor door, leading to the stairs to number 12, standing open. This was unusual, and Benstead climbed the stairs and found the door to his room half-open too. He went inside, and all was blackness but for Kitty's figure on the bed, silhouetted by the glow of the gas lamp outside. She was lying on her back with her boots still on, and fully clothed;

her skirt, however, had been lifted up, and its hem was at her neck. 'Kitty,' said Benstead, thinking that she was asleep. He went up to her and touched her on the shoulder.

Dark against dark, he saw blood on her lips and on the right side of her neck.

★

Down the stairs, left into the Court, through the archway, hard right, Benstead flew panicked through the door into John McCarthy's provision shop. John Day and Jeremiah O'Callaghan were there and Benstead, by his own account, gasped, 'Someone has done the old woman in!' O'Callaghan was, at the time, the occupant of Mary Jane Kelly's old room, number 13, a place haunted by the ghosts of murders past; now, he, Day and the agonised Benstead dashed up the stairs to number 12, to bear witness to the latest tear in the psychic fabric of Millers Court. In the darkness, O'Callaghan struck a match, and holding it up to Kitty's neck made out the blood; Day, looking on, thought he saw it still flowing from the wound. Kitty's eyes were wide open. O'Callaghan bent down and, putting his face near hers, believed that he felt her breathe, twice. He levered himself back up with his hand on the mattress, and touched a penknife, open and slick with wet blood, which he placed on the table. And then, perhaps trailed by a crowd of onlookers who had already caught hold of the commotion, Benstead went to the Commercial Street police station and reported the crime, while O'Callaghan and Day waited in the dismal room with Kitty perfectly motionless on the bed.

A small mob of policemen now filed in on the scene – Inspector Thomas Travis and PC Harry Baker, who were stopped in Duval Street by a lad who had picked up on the local excitement; Herbert Bursted, who had left PC Baker on the corner of Crispin Street and Duval Street at half past one, when all was quiet and still; a constable named Stevens, apparently summoned from Scotland Yard; an H-Division Sub-Divisional Inspector named Hammett; PC Harry Woodley, who drew a plan of the room, the Court, and the stretch of Commercial Street running parallel and to the east of the murder scene; and, shortly after two o'clock in the morning, 'in consequence of a telegram' sent to Leman Street police station, the redoubtable Detective Inspector Frederick Wensley. Wensley's *curriculum vitae*, when he finally retired in 1929, was a catalogue of many of the most famous criminal cases of his age. He had chased the shadow of the Ripper in 1888 as a fledgling constable; he would rescue a stricken colleague from anarchist gunfire at the Siege of Sidney Street; arrest Steinie Morrison for the murder of Leon Beron; secure the misspelled written evidence that hanged Louis Voisin; and, for better or worse, steer the investigation which brought Frederick Bywaters and Edith Thompson to the gallows for the murder of Edith's husband Percy. It was a stellar record, unmatched by almost any other officer. Wensley was always a man given to swift action, even after a series of promotions had nudged him out of the East End and into the tidier desk jobs available at Scotland Yard; sometimes, according to one assessment of the man, this blurred with a too-forceful attitude in dealing with hot situations. But he could also be meticulous and thoughtful. In the claustrophobic haze of the now-candlelit 12 Millers Court, Wensley was the only person to notice that Kitty's left hand – tucked under her body as if, in her last moments, she had attempted to conceal it there – clutched a penny. When the hand

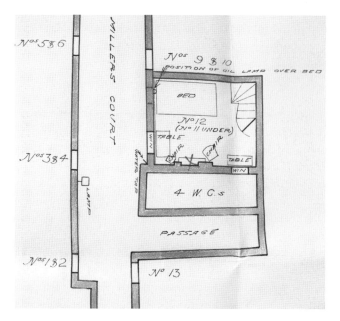
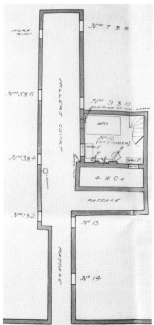

The drawings of Millers Court produced by PC Henry Woodley, showing Kitty Roman's bedroom and the house. (The National Archives, ref. CRIM 1/115/1)

was moved, the penny dropped onto the bedclothes. It was a gothic measure of Kitty's straitened circumstances.

The inquest into Kitty Roman's death opened on Saturday 3 July with an identification and the medical evidence. Percy Clark, the Police Surgeon attached to H-Division, had attended the scene in the aftermath of the discovery of the body, finding the body supine, with the head inclined to the left side. The left leg was bent at the knee, and its ankle lay under the right calf in a parody of what in life would have resembled relaxed confidence. On the right side of the neck, commencing an inch and a half below the angle of the jaw, there was an incised wound, and this wound continued round to the midline. It was 2.5ins deep, hacked out by a blunt blade, and Clark observed that it 'had divided the windpipe and the large vessels and nerve' on that side. Blood had spewed out, soaking the linen on the bed. More blood had bubbled from Kitty's nostrils; her tongue protruded between her teeth; and her pupils were dilated: these were clear signs of strangulation. There was no blood on her hands, and no sign of a struggle. Clark found moist semen on Kitty's underwear, and also on 'a piece of blind' which had doubled as a towel, and which had been left on a chair near the south-facing window. Following this initial examination, the body was removed to the Stepney Mortuary, but a post-mortem revealed little more: Kitty had eaten fish and potatoes before she died; it was found that her lungs had flooded with blood in the moments after her throat was cut. 'In my opinion,' Clark told the Coroner, Wynne Baxter, 'the injury was not self-inflicted, [and] it must have caused almost instantaneous death... I should say the injury had been inflicted at least an hour before I saw the deceased.'

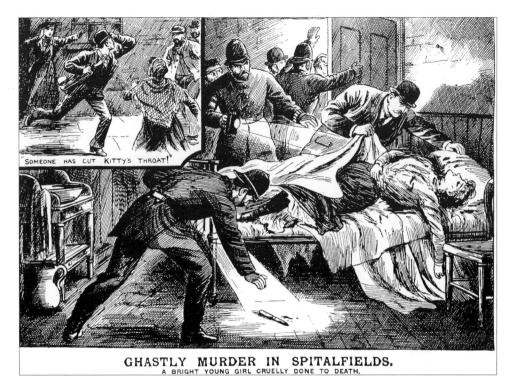

A depiction of the scene in Kitty Roman's room. (*The Illustrated Police News*, July 1909; courtesy of Robert Clack)

Clark's conclusion – instant death occurring at one o'clock in the morning – probably put the lie to John Day's feeling that he had seen blood issuing from the neck wound, and to Jeremiah O'Callaghan's impression that he had felt Kitty breathing: she had, most likely, been dead all along. It also exonerated Henry Benstead, but there were nine nervy days between the inquest hearings, and, during this time, the police's gaze, he knew, began to fix upon him. No other suspect had emerged to occupy their thoughts: a couple of shadowy, unidentified figures had been seen in Duval Street in the hours before the murder, but this was hardly unusual, and crumbs of this sort offered little solace to the thwarted detectives. So had Kitty died in a domestic incident? When the inquest resumed, on Monday 12 July, Benstead anxiously ensured that Tom Stanton and Barnet Sheinisohn were in attendance to testify to the fact that he was sitting quite innocently in the kitchen of the Bee Hive at the moment of his *inamorata's* brutal death.

Frederick Wensley's patience, in the meantime, was being gravely tested by the stalled criminal investigation. 'I had searching enquiries made,' he said at the inquest, 'and statements taken of every one who it was thought could throw any light on the matter. Up to the present no one has been charged.' This was a clipped, frustrated synopsis of the police's helplessness to solve the case. The Coroner's jury had no option but to find a verdict of 'murder against some person or persons unknown', and, a mere ten days after Kitty's death, the matter already seemed as if it might defy any more satisfactory conclusion.

Princelet Street, north side; the Bee Hive stood out of shot to the left. (Author's collection)

★

On the fine, fair evening of Sunday 18 July, Sergeant Sidney Rickards was at work in the charge office of the Central police station in Bristol. A man approached him, appearing worn, starved, untidy, and vexed, and confessed to the murder of Kitty Roman. Rickards alerted Wensley by telegram, and Wensley arrived in Bristol the next day.

The man in custody was one Harold Hall, who told Wensley that he had determined 'to act like a man' after seeing the case reported in the newspapers; now, he meant to 'see it through'. 'I want to tell you how it happened,' he said. Wensley cautioned Hall: he would have to report any of the prisoner's remarks. 'I want you to,' said Hall. 'I haven't any friends here.'

By his own account, Hall had been born into poverty in what he called 'Strangeways Workhouse' – a dismal institution standing in the shadow of Manchester Victoria Station, and steps away from the dark edifice of the famous prison. The destitution of Hall and his family attracted charitable pity, and, he said, 'me and my three brothers were sent away ... to Canada when we were children,' in anticipation of a happier existence. This was probably in the 1880s, and the event marked the start of Hall's epic peregrinations, which would end in miniature twenty years on as he tramped from London to Bristol with what he must have imagined to be his last free footfalls. In the meantime, a sailor's life had taken Hall 'all over the world', including to Johannesburg in South Africa, where he had been robbed of about £30 by a French prostitute. 'I didn't do anything to her,' Hall explained, 'but I made up my mind if it occurred again what I would do.' On 22 October 1908, he travelled to Liverpool from Spain aboard the steamship *Thelma*, working his passage over, and then stowed away on another boat to London. He spent some time in the Seaman's Hospital in Greenwich with a 'rupture', and then found his way to the Salvation Army Shelter on Spa Road in Bermondsey, leaving there on the afternoon of 1 July 1909 possessed of a broken penknife, which he had been using to break the bindings of books. During this time, he had been using the alias William Johnson.

On this fatal day, Hall walked to the East End, and passed the evening in the Shoreditch Empire. Emerging at a quarter to eleven, he had a few drinks and, on his way south down Commercial Street, encountered Kitty Roman. She encouraged him to return with her to her room: he consented. They stepped into the darkness of 12 Millers Court, and Hall removed his jacket and waistcoat. He asked her to put the gas on, but Kitty said there was none, and suggested that he light a candle instead. Hall struck a match, turned, and saw Kitty with her hand inside his coat pocket. Memories of Johannesburg flooded back.

'Is that your game?' demanded Hall. He 'flew at her in a rage', he said, 'caught her by the throat, threw her on the bed, held her there, she never spoke.' He drew his knife, opened the blade with his teeth, and plunged it into her neck. Fear suddenly washed over him, and he dropped the knife on the bed, and swept up his jacket and waistcoat, putting them on before leaving the court. Then he fled to the Queen Victoria Seamen's Rest Home on Jeremiah Street in Poplar, where, according to the porter, he booked two beds, one in the name of William Johnson, and the other in the name of Maloney. Hall had arrived at the Rest Home at half past one in the morning, just as the corpse of Kitty Roman was being discovered by Benstead, lying inert on the bed. The next day, Hall set out on his aimless march across the country. He entered the Stapleton Workhouse, on the outskirts of Bristol, on 14 July. Four days later, he confessed, and, back in London in the custody of Wensley, saw the knife which had been found on Kitty's bed. 'That's my knife,' he said.

Hall's confession seemed incontrovertible, but he had been unnecessarily coy about having had sex with Kitty – there seems little doubt that the semen found on her underwear was his, and that her attempt to rob him had occurred after they had slept together. Even at the time, Wensley must have considered it odd for Hall to talk so demurely about sex, but so candidly about murder. The internal corroboration of the story, however, was impeccable. Hall had admitted reading about the case in the newspapers, but Wensley carefully calibrated his confession against the facts which the press had given out.

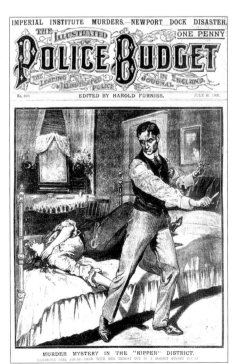

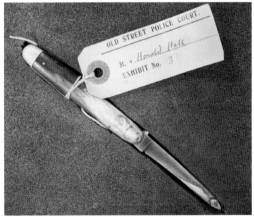

Above: Harold Hall's knife. (The National Archives, ref. EXT 11/133)

Left: Harold Hall re-imagined. (*The Illustrated Police Budget*, 10 July 1909; courtesy of Robert Clack)

Alcoholism was endemic in the East End of the Victorian era. Here, customers are being served 'through the window' on Whitechapel Road.

As far as Wensley could tell, none of the reports had described Kitty's room as being on the first floor, but Hall knew that it was. None had mentioned the strangulation attested to by Dr Clark, but Hall had described catching Kitty by the throat. The broken second blade of the penknife had not been publicised, but Hall was aware of it anyway. The details Hall had given of the absence of gaslight, and of the location in the room of the candles, and the proximity of the mantelpiece to the bed, all tallied, and nobody but the murderer could have described them. The decision to book a second bed at the Seamen's Rest Home smacked of misdirection – in his hurry, Hall was establishing a misleading trail of identities, hoping to distance himself from the crime. But he still used his recent alias, Johnson; and the fictional Maloney, in whose name Hall had booked the second bed, failed to turn up, as fictional characters are wont to do. Without his confession, it is likely that Hall would never have been caught, but Wensley perceived Hall's amateur, unpolished approach to the concealment of his crime, and, when the story came out, it was because Hall was, finally, tormented by the psychological consequences of his moment of anger. Hall was no criminal mastermind, and, when he presented himself to Sergeant Rickards at Bristol, it was an act tantamount to suicide – Hall had reached the nadir of his rambling, unsatisfying existence, and saw no point going on.

At his trial, held at the Old Bailey in September 1909, he was defended by Henry Devenish Harben only at the insistence of the court. In a spasm of last-minute nervousness, Hall had opted to plead not guilty, effectively retracting his statement to Wensley, despite its evident earnestness and the telling details it contained. Harben, in his turn, remarked on the proclivity of disenfranchised loners to confess to crimes they had not committed, but the jury found the evidence tying Hall to the murder to be watertight. He was found guilty, and was removed to Pentonville to await his execution, nodding his thanks to Harben on his way out of court.

★

The Queen Victoria Seamen's Rest Home, in Jeremiah Street, Poplar. (Author's collection)

Frederick Wensley wrote his memoirs in 1931. In his book, *Forty Years of Scotland Yard*, he recalled the Kitty Roman case. After Hall's conviction, Wensley felt obliged to ensure that the Home Office understood the real context of the crime. He obviously felt some compassion for Hall, whose life had been rough, who had been animated by a poorly-formed fantasy of vengeful omnipotence after his experience in Johannesburg, and whose plea at the Old Bailey had revealed, after all, a desire to live. Nineteen days after the verdict, Wensley remembered, 'I was summoned to the Home Office to give my views in person. That day the man was reprieved and I must admit that a load was taken off my mind.' One modern description of this sympathetic act has confused Wensley's humane sincerity with a secret desire to calm his supposed doubts about the security of Hall's conviction.

But Wensley had no such doubts. No capital case in Edwardian England was treated lightly, and Hall was not the only convicted murderer to have his sentence reduced to life imprisonment. Juries were deeply and seriously aware of their moral and civic duties to prisoners on capital charges. *Contra* the evidence, it has been said that the police, by the time of the trial, 'had grave doubts as to whether they had the right man'. This is untrue. It has been claimed that 'it was never conclusively established that the penknife was indeed the murder weapon'. This is specious. It has been suggested that the evidence against Hall was 'very flimsy'. This is misleading.

It is true that one of the prosecution witnesses, Alfred Wilkins, who had seen Kitty Roman going into Millers Court at midnight with a man resembling Hall, was, by September 1909, in custody awaiting his own trial for street robbery. Wilkins got four months' hard labour, but his obvious weaknesses as a prosecution witness did not undermine the factual foundation of his evidence. He had identified Hall in a line-up on 27 July, having previously, at a quarter past five in the morning on 2 July 1909 – that is, a matter of hours after the body was discovered – provided them with a description of the mysterious stranger, from the details of which he never deviated. The description, of a man standing 5ft 7ins tall, with a dark complexion, a dark moustache, a dark suit and a certain military bearing, was Hall's, at least prior to his whiskery trek across the English countryside. Wilkins also saw Hall leaving Millers Court some time between 12:15 and 12:20 a.m. – in their minutes together, Hall and Kitty had had sex, and he had strangled her and cut her throat. Unreliable though he may have appeared, Wilkins's testimony dovetailed perfectly, and naturally, with the other evidence in the case. The simple reason for this is that he was telling the truth; the corollary is that Hall's conviction was never unsafe.

In 1929, in the last months of his career, Wensley apparently received a visit from a man he had not seen in twenty years. This was Hall, who had, seemingly, been released from prison during the First World War and, Wensley said, 'served in France and elsewhere with distinction, reaching, I think, the rank of sergeant'. Hall thanked Wensley for his representations against the capital sentence. Wensley was flattered: 'I was able to give him an opportunity to earn a living in a decent way,' he wrote. The truth of the story is difficult to prove, but it should at least stand as an intriguing afterword to the tale of the death of Kitty Roman.

TWO SCENES IN WHITECHAPEL.

Seven

1911

The policemen and the soldiers rattled into their positions, all capes and antique rifles, stiff-limbed, their movements accelerated first by the firefight, and then by the ticking of the film. Special Branch lit their pipes, sent clouds of smoke camouflaged into the grey sky, and fastened their greatcoats against the winter chill. Women and children were urged back into their houses; men stood in clusters at either end of the street, their curiosity intensifying with every crack of a bullet against the brickwork, or worse. Churchill had himself chaperoned into prime position, forgetting himself, and, from beneath his top hat, gestured importantly at things. Somewhere nearby, trams clattered past the advancing Maxim Gun, awoken from its dreamless slumbers and ready for action.

Then flames crashed through the windows of the besieged building, and the battle was lost and won in the moment the gunfire fell into silence. Now, the noise was elsewhere: the fire engine came, and brought the escape; the crowds were forced back again as the inferno whipped up. Sidney Street was crowned with smoke, Special Branch watching in miniature imitation as the building offered itself, finally, to the fire. Inside, two bodies lay, disfigured in ashes. It was an inauspicious start to 1911.

Yards of rapid-fire images clattered through the picture houses – on the screen, the viewer now joined the military, the police, and the Home Secretary as they busied themselves in bringing down the last surviving members of a gang which had lately married their anarchist aspirations to a seemingly counter-revolutionary desire for conventional wealth, to be obtained at almost any cost. A raid on a jewellery shop in Houndsditch had finished bloodily; the victims of the gang's violence had been policemen; public indignation flared. The fact that the gang was made up of immigrants to the crucible of the East End had not escaped notice. England, it was said by one Member of Parliament, was an open door to 'the scum and riff-raff of Europe'; jurists pontificated about the fissures in the Aliens Act; one correspondent, writing to The Times, feared that riots would sweep through East London, unchecked by a police force now too weak to contain the surge of popular feeling.

The Jewish Chronicle, *meanwhile, rejected the idea that simplistic solutions could be found to complicated problems, and, instead, looked overseas. The immigration question originated not with the successes or failures of English law, it said, but in 'the Government offices in St. Petersburg'*

Churchill at the scene of the siege.

★

– *repressive Mother Russia. This was a point likely to resonate with the great, displaced Eastern European communities of Aldgate, Spitalfields, Whitechapel and St George in the East; but the stigmatising side-effects of the anarchist outrage were impossible to ignore, and, as the Gregorian year loomed ahead, there must have been a general desire for a little peace...*

Myer Abramovitch, too, hoped for a little peace. Headaches began to trouble him in the summer of 1911. He mentioned them to an acquaintance of his, Lazarus Rickman, who advocated a visit to a physician, but, privately, and to mutual friends, Lazarus thought that Myer looked ... not confused, exactly; nor miserable; but, rendering his impressions in his best English, as if he 'had got no money ... out of work ... he ain't got no pluck'. Myer would stand, distracted, Rickman said, and 'messing around with his head, like this'.

As Rickman suggested, work was indeed running scarce for Myer. An itinerant fruit seller by trade, he bought apples, oranges and bananas from a dealer in Hanbury Street and sold them on at an inevitably minimal profit – pennies, perhaps, here and there. Vast riches were permanently out of Myer's reach; and, recently, even liquidity had eluded him. In August 1909, and passing under the name of Mark Abrahams, he was convicted of a petty larceny – stealing fruit – and he had obtained seven other minor convictions for obstruction. At his lodgings at 5 Underwood Street, he slept in the same room as Emanuel and Harry Beckdanoff, two of the six children of Rose, the landlady. Before

December 1911 rolled around, the Beckdanoffs had almost certainly announced their intention to sail for South Africa; Myer, who had lived with the family for about two and a half years, would be required to find fresh quarters. He would also be expected to settle his debts with Rose: he had fallen behind on his rent to the tune of thirty-six shillings.

Funds had also dried up for Solomon and Annie Milstein. Their restaurant, located in the front parlour at 62 Hanbury Street, a little east of the junction with Brick Lane, depended largely on the patronage of the workers from a boot factory standing opposite. In the autumn of 1911, however, the workers left on strike, and, by the end of November, the dispute remained unresolved. The Milsteins' custom evaporated, and Solomon was forced to economise. Earlier in the year, they had retained a servant, living on the premises, to assist in the business; now, this was an expense too far. He may also have considered finding another situation for Cissie, Annie's eight- or nine-year-old orphan half-sister, who lived with them. Eventually, however, he alighted, in his desperation, on perhaps the worst of his options, and gave over his basement front room, below the restaurant, to an unlawful gambling club, of which he would be the inexperienced steward.

This was a partial solution to the cashflow difficulties which he and Annie had encountered – faro was played at threepence a round, paid by the participant holding the bank, and a five-shilling weekly levy for the use and occupation of the tight, airless room was also imposed. The financial bottleneck opened slightly, but Annie was unhappy about the noise, the number of players – more than a dozen, sometimes – and, she said, the type of men who were enjoying Solomon's hospitality. She spoke to her sister Fanny Herscowitz about her worries, and Fanny spoke to her husband, Lewis. A couple of weeks before Christmas, Lewis went to Hanbury Street to discuss the situation with Solomon, but Solomon brushed away Lewis's well-meant threat to take the matter to the authorities. The police, Solomon bluffed, were aware that gambling was taking place at the restaurant, but it was not for profit, so they were not prepared to do anything about it.

The innocence of Solomon's portrayal of his enterprise probably foundered on his admission that he had already acquired one partner, and that this partner hoped to bring in another – behind the sanitised language and the promises of rectitude, dark forces plainly lurked. The first of Solomon's partners, it seems, was one Jack Slovotinsky, who lived at 84 Hanbury Street; it was apparently he, in his turn, who tipped off Joseph Goldstein, a pugilist living at 168 Pelham Street Buildings, and fighting under the name of Joe Goodwin. Goldstein arrived at 62 Hanbury Street, offering his services as an enforcer, keeping order among the gamblers, and Solomon, backed further and further into a corner, offered him a cut of the takings. Annie, watching as Solomon lost control of his scheme, visualised an extortion-free life in America, and begged Lewis Herscowitz to intervene again. He did, visiting Solomon on Saturday 23 December 1911, and, this time, finding him sitting dejectedly apart from the throng of gathered punters. There was a small debt which Solomon wished to call in from one of the regular visitors to the gambling circle, but, he told Lewis, 'I have made my mind up to stop it next week'. Constitutionally, Solomon lacked what Lazarus Rickman might have called the *pluck* to manage an illicit gambling ring, and particularly one which had been infiltrated by racketeers and the professionally violent. Reassured by Solomon's change of heart, Lewis left the decommissioning of the gaming room to his brother-in-law.

The front of 62 Hanbury Street. (The National Archives, ref. CRIM 1/128/1)

The rear of 62 Hanbury Street. (The National Archives, ref. CRIM 1/128/1)

Solomon's resolve, though given to tremors, remained laudably intact for the next three days. On Boxing Day, he informed Slovotinsky that their arrangement was now at an end; Slovotinsky told Goldstein, and together they confronted their nervous partner. It was true, Solomon admitted: he had quarrelled with Annie about it, and she had insisted that the gambling cease. Goldstein accepted this blow to his own financial prospects with unlikely equanimity, advising the gamblers in the basement that the den was to be closed at the end of play that evening. By the time the games were completed, some time between half past midnight and a quarter to one on the morning of 27 December, only a handful of men remained. They were all ushered out of the restaurant at the same time, and Solomon Milstein rolled down the blind on the window at the front of the restaurant. The last profits of the venture were still to be divided – Slovotinsky and Goldstein would be back, probably no later than the next day, for their share of the spoils – but Solomon's unhappy expedition into the underworld of Spitalfields was coming, it seemed, to a tidy and opportune conclusion.

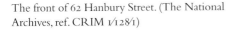

Above the Milsteins, on the first floor, live the Verbloot family. At the back of the premises, over the Milsteins' bedroom, Marks Verbloot – the eldest son, in his early twenties – sleeps in the same room as his mother. He wakes at about three o'clock on the morning of Wednesday 27 December and hears, distantly, the sound of a woman moaning, as if in pain. Marks rouses his mother and asks her to listen. They think the noise comes from the rooms above theirs; Mrs Verbloot says that one of the residents there suffers from hysteria. She goes back to sleep, but Marks lies awake, listening to the disturbing sound; and then, abruptly,

it stops, and there is silence. It is around half-past three — perhaps later, perhaps nearer four. Marks attempts to fall asleep. But now he smells smoke, and now he suspects that the Milsteins' rooms are on fire.

Marks wakes his mother again. He goes into the front room — above the restaurant — and speaks to his father. They look out of the window into Hanbury Street, and the fog is swirling down, but Mr Verbloot sees no fire. 'Don't be silly,' he says. 'You're dreaming.' Marks, however, is unconvinced, and, returning to the back room, he looks down towards the Milsteins' rear window; a light glows dimly, shapelessly, in the darkness of their bedroom. Marks takes a boot brush and leans out, aiming it at the window below his. It shatters one of the panes, and smoke pours through the aperture and twists into the night air.

Crashing back into the front room, Marks throws open his father's window and blows a police whistle which Mr Verbloot keeps in case of his own brushes with those who lurk in the shadows of Spitalfields. Then he rushes downstairs, through the Verbloots' separate exit to Hanbury Street, blowing the whistle again. Turning, he notices that the door to the Milsteins' restaurant stands

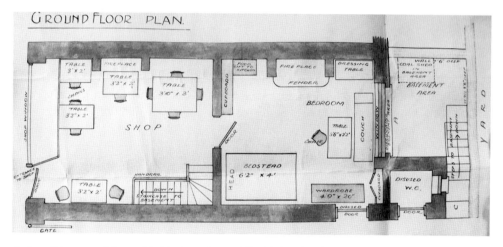

A plan of the ground floor of 62 Hanbury Street. (The National Archives, ref. CRIM 1/128/1)

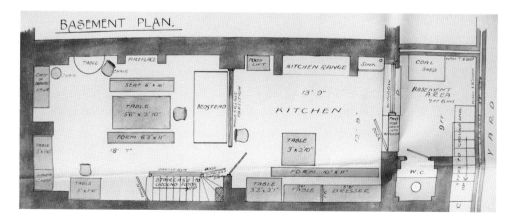

A plan of the basement of 62 Hanbury Street. (The National Archives, ref. CRIM 1/128/1)

wide open. Along the street, coming towards him, a policeman's lantern gleams softly through the near-sightless fog...

★

The next day, the gamblers who once frequented the dead couple's basement room began to identify themselves to the police. A little illicit faro below a failed restaurant was one thing; the threat of implication in a particularly ugly double murder, in the course of which the victims were stabbed, cut, beaten and, in Mrs Milstein's case, partially incinerated while still alive and perhaps no more than partly insensible – this was quite another. Far from coming from upstairs, Annie had indeed been the source of the moaning sound heard by Marks Verbloot – likewise, its sudden cessation probably meant that he had heard her die, giving in to her injuries, to haemorrhage, and to burns. In addition to the brutality of the manner of Annie's death, her killer had inflicted indignities apparently unconnected with his awful objective: she was found with her chemise rolled up around her neck, her belly having previously been incised through the fabric to the depth of about an inch; and the lower half of her body was found to have suffered worst in the fire, with the part most burned being the left groin. Solomon, by comparison, had suffered fewer obvious outrages, having seemingly put up a struggle against his assailant until a knife wound found the right lung, severing the bronchus, and incapacitating him almost instantly. Death, thought Percy Tranter Goodman, the surgeon who performed the autopsy, would have followed with little delay.

Harry Sojcher, a tailor's presser, had been one of those to announce himself to the police. He left the station at Leman Street at about one o'clock in the morning on 28 December, having gone there with (and perhaps at the insistence of) his landlady, Mrs Jons. On the way back towards their quarters in Corbett's Court, off Hanbury Street at the Commercial Street end, Sojcher saw Myer Abramovitch standing at a coffee stall outside Gardiner's department store. Harry recognised Abramovitch as a sometime patron of Solomon Milstein's gambling club. 'Here is Myer,' said Sojcher to Mrs Jons: at the coffee stall, Abramovitch looked up, saw Sojcher, and began shuffling slowly, deliberately away along the Commercial Road. 'Myer, Myer!' called Sojcher, crossing the road, and catching up with Abramovitch before he had gone very far. We are at the mercy of Sojcher's own English rendition of his original Yiddish in what happened next.

'Where were you all day?' asked Sojcher. 'All the people what was with Milstein give evidence at the Police Court. Where you were? You were the one that don't go to the police station. What is the matter with you that you don't go? Why don't you give evidence?'

Abramovitch said nothing to this.

'Come to the police station,' urged Sojcher, by his own description feeling, 'excited because very frightened.'

Still there was no response.

'Don't be afraid,' said Sojcher. 'Come with me.'

Through the night to Leman Street police station went a passive Abramovitch, impelled by the agitated Sojcher, whose nervous enthusiasm finally drove him on in front of his charge, reaching the desk of Inspector John Freeman alone. 'Where is Mr Wensley?' asked Sojcher, urgently. 'Myer is just up the road.'

'Is he wanted?' asked Freeman.

'Yes,' said Sojcher. 'The police have been looking for him all day.'

'What? In connection with the Hanbury Street murder?'

'Yes.'

Freeman took his cape and went to the door. Glancing up the road, he saw Abramovitch heading for Great Alie Street in the company of three women. Freeman raced after them. 'Myer,' he said, stopping his quarry, 'I want you.'

'Eh?' retorted Abramovitch, dully.

'I think you are wanted. Come with me to the station, will you?'

'All right,' replied Abramovitch, by now swept along on whichever tide took him, and together they set off for the station. Abramovitch had both his hands thrust deeply into the pockets of his coat, and Freeman, peering at him in the darkness, intuited that this was more than just a gesture of annoyance at the inconvenience of having to go to the police station.

'What is the matter with your hand?' enquired Freeman.

'I've cut it,' said Abramovitch, blankly.

They arrived at the station, where this was proved to be true. Abramovitch sported a great bandage on his left hand, dressed 'as if surgically', Freeman thought. To Frederick Wensley, hurriedly summoned to Leman Street, Abramovitch expanded – slightly – on his explanation of his injury. 'I got it cut in Hanbury Street this morning,' he said.

This was revealing, but more damaging discoveries were to follow. Abramovitch scarcely seems to have troubled to conceal the array of deeply suspicious items in which he was draped. Two watches he volunteered to Wensley, saying, 'I know what you want – you will find it in this pocket,' and these were proved to have been deposited with Solomon Milstein by a couple of his gamblers, ones who had hit upon costly losing streaks: a day later, and Solomon would have alchemised gold into cash, keeping the wolves – or Slovotinsky and Goldstein – at the door. The theft linked itself unambiguously to the murder, and the tragic timing of the incident suggested that the guilty party had learned of Solomon's determination to wind up his gambling ring: if the murder-theft initiative had once been little more than a nebulous dream of demonic character, the darkness at the heart of one of the restaurant's erstwhile customers, then the proprietor's delayed exhibition of wisdom had probably whipped it fatally into shape. Abramovitch had not been in the basement when Goldstein delivered the news of the closure of the gaming club, but it seems likely that he had received the news some other way. Solomon himself may have mentioned it privately – Abramovitch was one of the Milsteins' less imposing guests, not obviously aggressive or in dispute with the law, at least not day-to-day. When not playing faro, mainly through lack of funds, he was sometimes to be found sitting to one side, playing patience. He had also been an acquaintance of relatively long standing, and their association dated to the Milsteins' more prosperous years, prior to the strike at the factory. In sum, there may have been trust, perhaps prompting Solomon to reveal his plan to quit to Abramovitch separately. Still, the precise nature of the relationship evaded popular understanding. Harry Sojcher had seen Milstein being friendly towards Abramovitch, but he was guarded as to whether this goodwill was reciprocated.

Inside 62 Hanbury Street – the interior of the bedroom, looking towards the restaurant. (The National Archives, ref. CRIM 1/1281/1)

From his right-hand trouser pocket, Abramovitch took a purse, handing it to Wensley. 'This is his,' he muttered. 'You'll find all the money in there.' Wensley shook out £2 10s in gold, the last, scant proceeds of Solomon Milstein's illicit enterprise. But this was not all. Below the greatcoat, Abramovitch had assumed the costume of the deceased Solomon. He unwrapped in layers, the coat, and the suit below it, being Milstein's; below that, a second suit – Abramovitch's own – was stained with blood, and the blood had reached the underclothing. The bodies of the Milsteins had been discovered in their bedroom, and both had undressed for bed before the attack – Solomon's suit was probably hanging in the wardrobe, or perhaps lying on the dressing table, and taken after the killings. It was December, and the perpetrator of the crime may have been feeling the cold. Interpreted as a measure of desperation, the theft of the suit chimed with Abramovitch's own disheartened confession to the murders of the Milsteins: 'I done it because I lost all my money at gambling,' he reported.

★

With the Milstein killings, the grand-scale, even international, social effects of the Siege of Sidney Street were replicated at the molecular level – individual suffering bred

Inside 62 Hanbury Street – the interior of the restaurant, looking towards the bedroom. (The National Archives, ref. CRIM 1/1281)

individual desperation, and murder replaced mutiny as the *modus operandi* of the body apolitic. There were echoes of other cases, too. Like Lipski before him, Abramovitch appeared to have surrendered inertly to life's difficulties, eventually committing an act of terrible violence for advantages so slight as to be insignificant. In the course of the day after the killings, he had made no known attempt to rid himself of the spoils of his spree in the Milsteins' bedroom (excepting one small payment, chipping a few shillings off his debt to his landlady), and, when he was seen by Harry Sojcher, he stood at the top of one road with a police station on it, and at the bottom of another. His whole attitude seemed to speak of a detached indifference, the state of mind of one whose resilience had holed below the waterline. His body, as he brought it from the cells to the Police Court the next morning for the inspection of the waiting journalists, told the same squalid story. He was twenty-four or twenty-five, unkempt, with longish, untrained hair and a few days' growth of stubble on his chin. Denuded of his stolen trappings, he cut an impoverished figure in the dock, wearing no collar on his shirt, and with trousers which stopped stubbornly short of the ankles. At subsequent hearings, running through the January of 1912, Abramovitch appeared dejected, although he listened carefully as the case against him was presented. The wound on his left hand ceased to trouble him, and at length he discarded his bandage.

At the Old Bailey, in a two-day trial commencing on Wednesday 7 February 1912, the grim methods of the Milsteins' murders revealed themselves tier by tier, mirroring the way in which their self-confessed perpetrator had uncloaked himself from within layers of Solomon Milstein's bloodstained clothing. The fire which had damaged Annie's body had been catalysed by paraffin, and a squat bottle, itself marked with blood and nearly empty, had been found in the bedroom. A widow named Ruth Montgomery had been employed by Mrs Milstein as a domestic assistant in late November, perhaps at or around the time when the demand for meals – for better or worse – picked up incidentally to the formation of the gambling circle. Mrs Montgomery told the court that the bottle was not indigenous to the household; she would buy paraffin for some household tasks, she said, but in a comparatively taller vessel, produced in evidence. The fire, then, seemed to have been started by an offender bringing his own accelerant; Abramovitch, meanwhile, had been seen wearing a blue neckerchief at 7:00 p.m. on the fatal evening, and this neckerchief – or one indistinguishable from it – had also been left at the scene. It stank of unfired paraffin; and, though their emigration prevented the fact from coming out in direct testimony at Abramovitch's trial, the Beckdanoffs, the prisoner's host family in the years before the murder, kept their paraffin in a bottle in plain sight in their back yard. Harry Beckdanoff knew Abramovitch to have amassed a small collection of squat bottles, which he kept on the mantelpiece or under his bed. Normally, Harry said, Abramovitch filled them with rum, and then drained them in the usual escapist manner.

Appearing in Abramovitch's defence, Arthur Woolf Elkin jabbed artlessly at the evidence of the prosecution witnesses. With the case against his client becoming increasingly coherent, he ushered the court's attention away from the damaging realities and towards trivia. This tested the patience of the judge, Mr Justice Ridley: on the second day, Elkin asked Harry Sojcher exactly where he had parted from Abramovitch on their jumpy journey to the police station. 'Do you think that is important?' enquired Mr Ridley.

'It is rather important, my Lord,' said Elkin, earnestly.

'Then put the question. Put anything you like,' sighed Mr Ridley.

'It was just at two or three houses before the corner of Great Alie Street and Leman Street,' said Sojcher.

'That does not matter a bit,' said Mr Ridley.

Other lines of defence suffered equally through Elkin's disjointed cross-examinations. *Passim*, he had urged the court towards a consideration of Abramovitch's mental health, but, by the end of the case for the prosecution, the prisoner's madness was far from proved. Some witnesses had specifically rebuffed the idea that Abramovitch could have been irresponsible for his actions – Elkin had suggested to the Divisional Surgeon Percy Clark, for example, that anyone wearing many layers of clothing might be considered insane. Clark observed patiently that some people in Whitechapel wore three coats, and implied that they did so for no reason more sinister than that they were often cold. 'Do you think everybody is insane in Whitechapel?' Mr Justice Ridley asked Elkin, slightly contemptuously. 'I am putting the question seriously.'

In the end, the prosecution called Dr Sidney Reginald Dyer, the senior medical officer at Brixton Prison, where Abramovitch had been held on remand. After a cursory

The grave of Solomon and Annie Milstein. (Author's collection)

Part of the inscription on the Milsteins' grave. (Author's collection)

examination in which he described his contact with the prisoner, he eliminated Elkin's theory with something approaching condescension: 'We have at Brixton a very large number of persons come in every year,' he said, 'and you would be surprised at the large number who come in with three, four, five and six suits on.'

Elkin spared his doomed client the trauma of giving evidence in his own defence. The jury retired at ten minutes past one on the second afternoon, returned after ten minutes' consideration, and found Abramovitch guilty. 'Thank you, sir,' said Abramovitch, speaking through a veil of tears as the judge condemned him to death. Two warders held him up as his nerve broke.

★

On 19 February 1912, Abramovitch's appeal against his sentence was dismissed with perfunctory celerity. Arthur Elkin depended again on the arguments which had failed him at the Old Bailey, complementing these with spicy but insubstantial allegations of misdirection on the part of Mr Justice Ridley. From the bench, Mr Justice Channell disposed of Elkin's inelegant legal mishmash without calling on the counsel for the Crown, and the date of Abramovitch's execution was fixed for 6 March 1912.

Even before his appeal had been heard, Abramovitch had apparently confessed his guilt to a friend of his named Davis Byer. Byer visited Abramovitch as he sat counting down the days in Pentonville Prison, and Abramovitch said that he had waited a fortnight to have the chance to commit the murders. On Boxing Day, Cissie Barr, the Milsteins' young ward, went to visit one of Annie's sisters, perhaps intending to stay for a few nights, and Abramovitch interpreted this as his cue to act. On the fatal night, with Solomon downstairs eyeing the gamblers and Annie out of the house on an errand, Abramovitch got into the Milsteins' bedroom, hid under their bed, and waited his moment. He was there nearly an hour and a half, he believed, emerging only after the restaurant had closed and when he thought the couple were soundly asleep above him. Byer reported this conversation to Frederick Wensley a day or two after it had taken place; Wensley sent the tale on to the appropriate authorities. Against this version of the sad events, however, was the statement of principal warder of the prison, who had been sitting in on Abramovitch's interview with Byer and who remembered no such confession. Abramovitch may indeed have gone into his last weeks still burdened by the dark truth, unable to confide in Byer or, indeed, in anybody else. A self-protective layer had been wasted here and there in the course of the judicial proceedings against him, but it seems likely that the condemned man guarded some of his most closely-held secrets, however uselessly, to the very end.

In early March, John Ellis, the nation's hangman of greatest repute, travelled down from his Lancashire home to execute Abramovitch, detouring via the Old Bailey, where Frederick and Margaret Seddon were being tried for their part in the clumsy poisoning of Eliza Mary Barrow. The Seddons' case had captured the attention of the public, but, even against this tingling, distracting backdrop, Ellis recollected the murder of the Milsteins as a 'notorious' affair.

Beyond this remark, however, Ellis says nothing, and we are thrown upon the resources of our imagination for Myer Abramovitch's last moments. Of the last, fearful night spent in the condemned cell; of the solemn march to the scaffold; of the fitting of the cap and the noose: of none of these is there any word. Death, though, came to Abramovitch instantaneously, according to a disarmingly matter-of-fact report in *The Times*; the rope drew taut and still; *and there this reverie swirls swiftly away from us, with the living left above, and the dead suspended motionless below, the rhythm of the Kaddish arrested on the tongue of the Rabbi, and outside the little room a flash of sunshine and the smell of wet stone in the early spring.*